GLAD TO BE GREY

GLAD
to be
GREY

or

My Other Car's ALSO A Volvo

A Celebration of Dullness

PETER FREEDMAN

Cartoons by Ken Pyne

For all of us who aren't stylish, with-it, hip
chic, trendy, sparkling and fascinating –
and aren't worried about it.

ROUTLEDGE & KEGAN PAUL
London and Henley

First published in 1985
by Routledge & Kegan Paul plc

14 Leicester Square, London WC2H 7PH, England

and
Broadway House, Newton Road,
Henley on Thames, Oxon RG9 1EN, England

Set in 11 point Plantin
by Columns, Reading
and printed in Great Britain
by T.J. Press (Padstow) Ltd
Padstow, Cornwall

British Library Cataloguing in Publication Data

Freedman, Peter

Glad to be grey, or, My other car's also a
Volvo: a celebration of dullness.
I. Title
828'.91409   PR6056.R39/

ISBN 0-7102-0453-1
ISBN 0-7102-0756-5 Pbk

To my parents, whom I talked into buying their first Volvo, and
Fiona, with whom I one day hope to buy one myself

'May you live in interesting times.'
OLD CHINESE CURSE

'Because he was at that time the most
interesting man in Europe.'
Fascist leader, OSWALD MOSELEY, on being asked by a government
committee why he made such frequent visits to see Mussolini

'Trying to be fascinating is an asinine position to be in.'
KATHERINE HEPBURN

'It's natural to be dull. Mountains are dull. Flowers are dull.
Birds are dull. They don't hang around in bars trying to impress
people.'
J.D. 'DULL' STEWART

'Dullness! whose good old cause I yet defend,
With whom my muse began,
with Whom shall end.'
ALEXANDER POPE

Contents

Preface and Acknowledgments

Glad to be Grey is more than just the first style guide for the unstylish. And more than just the first celebration of the heroes and heritage of both the dull and very dull.

It is also a polemic, a rallying cry and a plea for tolerance. A statement of dull pride.

In a world obsessed with being interesting and a society hung-up on being hip, chic, with-it, stylish, sparkling and fascinating, it is a call on the dull and persecuted at last to take a stand. To Dare to be Square. To admit and not to care who knows it, 'Yes, My other Car's ALSO a Volvo'.

It is a call on all of us who happen to *enjoy* talking about the weather, to *like* the taste of English cooking and to *feel comfortable* in flared trousers, to stop apologizing for the fact.

A call, in short, on the dull-at-heart everywhere to come out and say, 'Glad to be Grey'.

Thanks to all those who helped make this book as dull as it is.

In particular to Stephanie Billen for doing the work, Ken Pyne for his memorably dull cartoons, Graeme Grant and Sean Paton for their valuable help and Fiona Halton and my family for all their support.

And especially to Philip Astell, Andrew Billen, *The Bookseller*, Craig Brown, Patrick Donovan, Julian Friedmann, Peter Hopkins, Philip Jenkinson, Bunny King, Peter Knight, Lael McCall, Graham Nonn (and his Oddfax library), Pendennis, Carole Price, Stephen Pile, Terry Quigley and Godfrey Smith.

As well as to the *Daily Telegraph* for permission to use an extract from its Peterborough column; Christopher Logue for permission to retell some of his *Private Eye* 'True Stories'; *The New Statesman* for permission to reprint extracts from 'This England'; Oxford University Press for permission to retell an anecdote from *A Long Retrospect* by F. Anstey (1936); and World Almanac Publications for permission to draw on material from their *Book of Buffs, Masters, Maverns and Uncommon Experts* (1980).

Peter Freedman, Kilburn, 1985

INTRODUCTION

THE MAN WHO ASKED FOR TOMATO KETCHUP IN LANGAN'S BRASSERIE
(After H.M. Bateman)

I'm OK.
You're a Little on the Dull Side

No doubt there has always been pressure to be interesting; a certain requirement to be stylish, with-it and chic. In the past, however, it was restricted to society's upper echelons of royal courtiers and salon stars, the cocktail cockatoos and relentlessly witty fops and dandies who were the brilliant guests of the brilliant hostesses. Plus the odd romantic poet, alienated artist or swash-buckling explorer.

But for the rest of us, dull was normal and we were happy.

Did Joe and Joanna Feudal-Serf, for instance, feel they had to hang around the ducking pond after a day at the plough or the lathe, and crack endless put-downs of Barry Manilow to show what a hip guy they were? Or did they just wiggle down to Ethelred's Wine Bar and fork out a year's Danegeld on a glass of imported mineral water?

Or, when Nelson blew the French out of the water at Trafalgar and staved off an invasion, did we tell him not to be so desperately uncreative, and have another croissant?

Or, when Hitler annexed the Sudetenland and marched into Poland did we say, 'Gosh, what a fascinating bloke, there's never a dull moment with that Führer', and dismiss it as a prank because he had once been to art school and was said to be a wow at mass rallies?

Or, even when Gandhi led India to independence did we write him off as a square because he didn't show on the day in a bondage loincloth and green mohican coif?

Not how I remember.

Dull is a four letter word

Today, though, things are different.

We live now in a society blighted by the ravages of designer mineral water and designer art students, video cafés and Porsche-driving rock stars, free-range travel writers and ubiquitous mime artists blocking the pavements and frightening the children with their over made-up faces and endless impressions of someone climbing up an invisible wall.

A society in which, whether or not we'd prefer a sausage roll and a week at home, we are expected to want foreign food and foreign holidays in faraway countries with unpronounceable names and undrinkable water.

A society in which, whether or not we'd *really* like a game of bowls and a cup of tea, we are pressured into dangerous sports and sipping white wine spritzers in overpriced wineries.

A society in which, whether or not we'd feel happier in a Burton's suit or St. Michael's cardigan, we are expected to shop at jumble sales and flea markets with real fleas for the cast-off clothes of complete strangers our mothballs would once have been insulted to share a cupboard with. Or else to squeeze into too tight clothes covered in strange animals and other people's names.

A society in which, to resist these pressures is to be labelled dull. And in which dull is a four letter word.

'Dullism' – The new snobbery

We live now in a society governed by the philosophy of 'I'm OK. You're a Little on the Dull Side.'

A society in which 'Dullism' – the wanton persecution of those deemed dull – has become the New Snobbery; with the question being no longer, 'Is she well born?' or 'Did he go to public school?', but, 'Does he know the difference between Nouvelle Cuisine and Cuisine Poseur?', or she, 'Between Gucci and Pucci?'.

At worst, the pressures can lead to the excesses of attention-seeking travel writers perpetually rounding Cape Horn in a coracle and crossing the Urals on a unicycle.

Or, more commonly, they are forcing even the formerly sane and solid into behaving like advertising creative directors and London

Weekend Television producers, forever straining and striving to keep up-to-date, au courant, à la mode, chic by jowl and pied à terre – victims on the modern altar of obsession with having an Interesting job, going Interesting places, being an Interesting person.

Boring is Not the Word – Dull, It Is

It is in this society that dull folks are the ones who say things like, 'Wohh there', and, 'Steady on'.

Things like, 'No, there's nothing like real margarine'. Though not like, 'I bet he's good in futon'.

They are maligned, beleaguered, put-upon folks who just because they don't climb on every bandwagon and join every fad are rated fair game for every square-basher and trendy-chops, short on the grey matter.

They are Wordsworth's 'plain-living, high-thinking' souls, persecuted by the Tyranny of Chic. The kind mocked by art students, turned away from nitespots and beaten up along the King's Road.

Dull folks are the honest, open sort who frankly admit to liking the music in supermarkets and lifts, the food on British Rail and the jokes in Christmas crackers. And who always ask for the recipe on aeroplanes.

They are the uncomplicated, straightforward types who genuinely prefer tap water to Perrier and sincerely believe that Frank Bough is 'a pretty snappy dresser'.

They are the folk who spot the emperor's designer clothes, and ask, 'So, what's wrong with "Man at C & A" all of a sudden?'

. Dull folks are the common citizen doing an honest day's work – the reliable, affable types who are kind to animals, help old ladies across the street and keep the show rolling on breakfast television.

They are the simple, upright souls for whom LA is short for Luton Airport, underground culture is the busking down the tube

and Alternative Theatre the one they went to that time they couldn't get into *The Mousetrap*.

They are the unhip, uncorrupted folks who still think of grass as what covers a lawn, coke as a soft drink, the Barbican as an alcohol-free lager and Covent Garden as somewhere they vaguely remember having heard of during a schools film about the fruit and vegetable industry for Geography O level in 1956.

Dull folks are not necessarily old or young, rich or poor, Left or Right. They are simply the low-key, down-to-earth kind who are realistic enough to know that life is not one long Martini commercial, tolerant enough to oppose capital punishment for the wearing of flared trousers or polyester suits, and secure enough to know that if you can keep your head while all around you are losing theirs and blaming it on you, you'll be written off as dull; but still not worrying about it.

Let's face it, most of us are dull

Dull folks are also the 99 per cent of us who never feature in the gossip columns or history books, never get pictured in perfume ads or profiled on *The South Bank Show*.

They are the average Joe's and regular gals, neither famous nor flash, who drill David Bowie's fillings, dry-clean Boy George's frocks, do David Hockney's accounts and deliver Joan Collins' mail.

They are the ordinary folk, neither glossy nor glittering, who drive our buses, hew our coal, tend our bunions and mop up our sick on cross-channel ferries.

They are the nobodies from nowheresville, the out-crowd with the Wrong Stuff, who know that, King Chicster, Andy Warhol *may* have said that in the future we will all be famous for fifteen minutes. But who also know that, apart from the fact that, how many of *your* friends have so far made the cover of *Newsweek?* – or even *Discount Freezer?* – for the average punter that still leaves 69 years, 365 days, 23 hours and 45 minutes of numbing obscurity.

And who know that the nearest most of us are going to get to fame is being paged on the office tannoy. Or having a letter to the editor published in *Condemned Veal Weekly*. Or maybe being lucky enough to meet a man who knew a man whose great aunt once heard the Queen sneeze. Or so she said.

Boring is not the word

The other thing to say is that dull does not mean stupid or boring.

Take, for example, Robert Oppenheimer, the misguided genius who led the research to develop the atom bomb. He was the sharpest mind of his generation. Yet, as an undergraduate, and at an age when classmates were out rocking round the clock and gang-banging the sorority girls, out running chamber pots up flagpoles and setting light to the college porter, all dull Bob could manage was a famous letter home, recording, 'It was so hot today the only thing I could do was to lie on my bed and read *Jean's Dynamical Theory of Gases*.'

Even Sir Geoffrey Howe-Dullcanyouget is no dunce.

As for boring, look no further than the Baron of Boredom himself, playwright, Samuel Beckett. His lifestyle – lives in Paris, knew James Joyce, almost certainly reads Proust – is pure anti-dull. He is the idol of anti-dulls everywhere. Yet his plays are titanically boring. To the point where there is little doubt that the best way to get people back into the theatres would be simply to stage more Beckett plays in the streets.

Wine snobs are boring; teetotallers are dull.

Of course, dull folks – like any folks – *can* be boring. But they are more often simply not particularly interesting, stylish, chic, sparkling or fascinating.

Could Oscar Wilde have been dull?

No, dull means simply having a more relaxed, easy-going approach to life.

Oscar Wilde, for example, would have been dull if, instead of his incessant witticisms about being able to resist anything but temptation and having nothing to declare but his genius, he had just once or twice eased off and admitted, 'I can resist anything but . . . fish fingers'. Or that, 'I have nothing to declare but . . . a carton of Rothmans and a six-pack of DayNurse.'

As it was, he was an insufferable too clever by half wit from whom it was impossible to get a straight answer.

Attila the Hun would have been dull if, instead of marauding across Europe, raping and pillaging, and putting women and children to the sword, he had taken a leaf from the Grand Old Duke of York and simply marched them down again. Let them work off their aggression like that. Or, if instead of invading Italy and Gaul, he had simply struck them off his Christmas card list.

As it was, he was the man of the moment, the face on every chat show and, no doubt, Radio Four's Man of the Year.

Or even Michelangelo would have been dull if, instead of spending all those years fine-detailing the frescoes on the Sistine chapel, he had nipped up a step ladder over a long weekend and slapped on a couple of coats of non-drip beige. Or else just covered the whole thing with . . . no, only an art student would cover a *ceiling* with lino.

Dull Folks Don't Write Travel Books – The Three Big Don'ts of Dull

The do's and don'ts of dull are many.

Ultimately, however, there are just three rules which sum up and symbolize everything dull folks aren't and would never want to be.

1 Dull folks don't write travel books

First, because dull folks don't write books. They may draft the odd postcard from Margate or thankyou note in reply to a thankyou note. But never something as interesting as a book. Let alone one called, *I Rode With the Bulgars East of Kathmandu.*

Second, because dull folks don't travel*. Of course, they commute back and forth to work. They may even sneak a package holiday to say, Mallorca (the built-up side) or a furtive listen to the long-range weather forecast. But you'd never catch a dull person on a trans-global expedition, crossing the Gobi Desert on a pogo stick or fording the South China Seas in a Squeezy bottle.

---

* What with not travelling much, dull folks don't speak many foreign languages either. Such so-interesting-they're-boring types as Peter Ustinov (international actor, writer, director, wit and raconteur) and Rudolph Nureyev (Tartar's peasant son, born on a train in Outer Mongolia, Kirov star, sometime defector and Artistic Director of the Paris Opera Ballet) for instance, speak a heap of them.

But take the case of travel writer, Ted Simon. (Simon, you won't need his publishers to remind you, rode his motorbike '63,000 miles and 54 countries round the world. Spinning through the Sudanese desert; into prison in Brazil; into the California commune; through wars, revolutions, disasters; into depths of despair,

If there is one country about which dull folks write fewest of all travel books, it must be China.

Dull folks all know that moment of combined embarrassment and incredulity when the conversation comes round to China and they have to admit that not only have they not written a single book about the place, but they've never even *been* there – not overland, not no how.

D.H. Lawrence, for instance, wrote travel books. Have you ever read one by Geoffrey Howe?

2 Dull folks never went to art school

(Few went to drama or mime school either, but none went to art school.)

If they went to college at all it was to read Chemical Engineering at Keele or Fish Technology at Hull Polytechnic or else Computer Programming at some northern outpost where the students all wore anoraks and polyveldt shoes and *went* to the lectures.

David Bowie, Bryan Ferry, Adam Ant all went to art school. Janet Street-Porter, could have been a professor. Sebastian Coe went to Loughborough University of Technology.

3 Dull folks don't drive Porsches

(Few drive BMWs, Lotus Esprits or white convertible VW Golf GTIs with white hubcaps either, but none drive Porsches.)

For, while in most areas of their lives, dull folks are middle-of-the-road, on the road itself, they stick to the slow lane. 'Never knowingly undertaken' is their motto.

---

heights of euphoria, and a fleeting love affair. Riding the tightrope across vast continents, meeting their peoples, he was seen as a spy, as a glamorous, astonishing stranger and as a deity. For Simon himself, it became a journey to the centre of his soul.')

Simon, apparently, speaks not only English, French, German, Spanish, a smattering of Arabic, Baha, Malaysian and Hindi but also two words in the Chinese Hokien dialect, meaning 'jolly good'.

'If he lives anywhere', add his publishers in a phrase which speaks a thousand travel books, 'it is in' (you've guessed it) 'France.'

But on the subject of cars, dull folks know only one thing. Which is that the next time they are tootling along a quiet back road in their Volvo Estate with front and rear crumple zones or old Hillman Imp with Go-Slower stripes, and some hot-shot wine-bar designer in a nail-lacquer red Porsche turbo comes vrooming round the bend like Emmerson Fittipaldi on Dexodrine, and, ignoring the 'Slow: Flooding' signs in his bid to break the world land speed all-comers record, gives a free bath to their freshly turtle-waxed bonnet . . . they know that, they will not loose their cool or honk, swear or chase.

Rather, they will merely keep calm and picture the result when one of these days, round another tight bend, the Porsche's push-button stereo jolts the answering machine on its Cellnet car phone into the backseat jacuzzi and short-circuits the electrically heated seats: one fried wine-bar designer.

George Harrison, for instance, drives a Porsche. Newsreader, Martyn Lewis drives a Volvo.

Are Men the Duller Sex as Well as the Uglier One? Notes Towards a Sexual Politics of Dullness

It would be insulting to suggest that women, too, cannot be dull. And foolish to claim that history has not known dull women.

It was, for example, a rare night – especially mid-week – that Queen Victoria disco danced till dawn.

And a rare day that Flo Nightingale went body-popping behind the supplies tent with the hipper members of the off-duty Light Brigade. On returning from the Crimea, indeed, she spent the remaining fifty-three years of her life in bed.

And, it was, after all, a woman who articulated the dullness of a generation, that moment when Doris Finsecker turned to a fellow student in the film of *Fame*, and wailed, 'EVERYONE ELSE HERE IS COLOURFUL, ECCENTRIC OR CHARISMATIC AND I'M JUST ORDINARY'.

And yet, there is no denying that men have historically been under far more pressure to be interesting. Grey Liberation and dull consciousness have in the first instance, therefore, grown out of an awareness of the pressures men in particular face to be thought interesting, clever, witty and amusing by women.

Men, today, as ever, point out dull thinkers, are forced to live up to female definitions of male fascination. We men are surrounded – on television, advertising, romantic fiction – by images of fascinating males: swashbuckling, adventurous men and suave, debonair men of easy charm; dark, mercurial men with unknown pasts and unknowable futures; brilliant dilettantes and chat-show raconteurs; millionaire rock stars with race-horses and yachts; poets, bohemians, travel writers . . . they are all around us.

You only want us for our bodies, women have told men. But men have never had it so simple. Men have had to be more than just a pretty face. Women have been chatted up. But men have had to do the chatting. In the past women were the brilliant hostesses. But it was men who had to be the brilliant guests, singing for their supper with ready banter and glittering repartee.

Even before the modern persecution of the dull, therefore, dull men have been a neglected species. While memoirs recall the brilliance of Oscar Wilde and his cronies adlibbing entire books of quotations round a table at the Café Royal, no record remains of the stumbling interjections of their less smart alec companions.

And while the Bloomsbury biographies remember the soirées dominated by Clive Bell and Lytton Strachey trading epigrams on Truth and Beauty to the delight of the female guests, not a footnote recalls the contributions of the less attention-seeking males making up the numbers on those interminable evenings.

It is only in recent years that women have begun to face similar pressures. To face the kind of harassment exemplified by a recent American magazine advertisement spotted by Jessica Mitford, which asked its potential female purchasers of a set of 'Great Books', 'The Women Your Husband Works With – Are You As Interesting As They?'

Now women, too, must be Interesting. It is the double-edged legacy of liberation.

The Great and the Dull –
Dulls Who Made Good

We expect certain things of our heroes – of the great men and women who have shaped history. They should be charismatic and, if possible, mercurial. Passionate, and occasionally brooding. House-proud of the soul while heedless of the body.

Or, at the very least, they should have . . . a flat in Chelsea, a job in the media and a distressed leather jacket in which to carry a crumpled pack of Gitanes (free gold earring with every carton).

How, then, do you account for the number of our all-time greatest statesmen and thinkers, artists and intellectuals, writers and poets who have in fact been profoundly dull people? Did you know, for instance, that:

* Franz Kafka (literary great) was an insurance clerk who chewed every mouthful of food a dozen times before swallowing?
* T.S. Eliot (Nobel Prize-winning poet and critic) was a banker who wrote the words for Andrew Lloyd-Webber's musical, *Cats*?
* Clement Attlee (founder of the Welfare State and National Health Service, and our greatest post-war prime minister) was said to have the charisma of a building society branch manager, and reminded George Orwell of 'nothing so much as a dead fish before it has had time to stiffen'?
* L.S. Lowry (our finest painter of this century) earned his living as a rent collector, and summed up the importance of Art and Beauty in a godless world with the aphorism, 'Art? All the art in the world isn't worth a good meat and potato pie.'
* James Joyce (Irishman and genius, hero of Parisian anti-dulls)

had the conversational range of a speak-your-weight machine? Truffles and headaches were his sole topics with Proust, as were parakeets with Le Corbusier.

★ Ludwig Wittgenstein (World Philosophers' XI) gave away his fortune to become an an elementary school teacher and didn't mind what he ate so long as it was always the same?

★ Philip Larkin (our leading poet) is a librarian who lives in Hull and doesn't go abroad for fear of missing the cricket scores? And who says, 'I lead a very commonplace life. Everyday things are lovely to me'?

★ Laurence Olivier (our greatest actor) has repeatedly insisted that privately he is a dull man and lacks any point of view? Confirms his wife, actress Joan Plowright, 'People would never believe how very *ordinary* he is at home'. Or that,

★ René Magritte (greatest of the Surrealist painters) lived in a trim house in suburban Brussels with his wife and a string of pet Pomeranian dogs?

No, you probably didn't know all this. Because the contribution of dullness to our civilization is these days a conveniently forgotten, if not well-kept, secret.

It's time, therefore, we began not just to recognize but to shout about the dullness of so many of our great figures – our *Eminences Grises* – and the contribution it made to their greatness.

In future chapters therefore, as well as documenting the dullness of ordinary men and women, we will be celebrating the ordinariness of the Great and the Dull.

The Royal and The Dull

In her book, *A Guide to Social Climbing*, social climber, Viviane Ventura dismisses our Princess Alexandra with the designation, 'Good but Dull' royalty. This, presumably, is as opposed to 'Tyrannical but Chic' royalty, such as Ivan the Terrible, Pedro the Cruel and Vlad the Impaler who, by all accounts, was a real card and great value at an impaling.

The point is, so many of history's greatest sovereigns have *not* been dashing, romantic figures, forever charging off on pointless crusades and ruinous adventures. Rather, they have been uninspiring but dependable types who have brought a steady hand to the tiller of government. Or who, like our own Queen, have preferred to stay home and do the *Daily Telegraph* crossword.

Indeed, of all the world's royal families is there, or has there ever been, one duller – and one prouder to be dull – than the British?

And would we want it otherwise? Would we *want* the Queen to show for the state opening of Parliament in a silver lamé boilersuit over pink denim hotpants? Or to open her Christmas broadcast to the Commonwealth with the words, 'My live-in-lover and I . . .'?

In any discussion of dull royalty special mention is due to:
– George V, both for never going abroad if he could help it and for always having lights out at precisely 11.10 p.m.
– Edward VIII, both for his passion for needlepoint and his prodigious collection of china dogs.
– Edward VII for articulating the footweariness of the Un-known Tourist by remarking after visiting Rome, 'You look at two mouldering stones and are told it's the temple of something.'
– George II for falling to his death from a lavatory seat.
– Henry VIII for his love of rhubarb.

And among modern royals:
– Princess Diana, both for her partialness to Twiglets and for winning, with a little help from her guinea pig, Peanuts, her school's coveted Palmer Cup for Pet's Corner.
– Prince Philip for confessing, 'My only tangible contribution to British life has been to improve the rear lights on lorries'.
– The Queen Mother both for being one of Perry Como's greatest fans and for confessing her favourite radio programme to be *Mrs Dale's Diary*.
– Prince Charles for his magnificent collection of lavatory seats.

The Grey Goose Awards for the World's Ten Dullest Folks

1 Sir Geoffrey Howedullcanyouget

Perhaps the dullest figure of his generation, and the dullest Foreign Secretary of any generation, Howe's name has become a byword for British dullness and the power of positive plodding.

As a public figure he has all the sparkle and panache of the Hush Puppies which are his favourite footwear.

Some politicians' speeches set their audiences alight; Howe's seem to be made of asbestos. It is a fact worth pondering that if Howe had led the rallies at Nuremberg, the last war would never have happened.

As journalist John Junor has asked:

> 'May it not in the long run pay dividends to have as foreign
> secretary someone who, far from arousing animosity in the hearts
> of foreigners, only makes them want instead to put a protective
> arm in his and guide him across a busy road?'

2 The Queen

Even by the standards of her own family, EIIR is an undeniably dull fish. Her dress sense – the epitome of Drab Chic – is admired by dull folks everywhere. Her annual Christmas broadcast to the Commonwealth is a dull highlight of any year, which only watching *The Great Escape* for the twelfth time afterwards can match. It is her dullness we prize her for.

Put it this way. Which of the following monarchs would you guess counted among their favourite music the score to *Oklahoma*, and their favourite foods, grilled haddock?

   a. The Emir of Cordoba?
   b. The Sultan of Zanzibar?
   c. The Pasha of Marrakech?
   d. The Grand Vizier of all the Mesopotamias?
   e. The Queen of Sheba?
   f. The Queen of England?

3 Michael Jackson

Young, gifted and dull – the biggest music superstar in the world and probably also the dullest. As a Jehovah's Witness (one of the world's great dull religions) Jackson doesn't drink, smoke, take drugs or swear. So, while other rock stars are splashing out on ivory coke spoons and gold-plated Lamborghinis (all the better to drive into the hotel swimming pool), oysters and Bollinger, his idea of a good time is tucking into a piled plateful of his favourite food, frozen custard, or indulging his only real vice – a passion for fresh carrot juice.

Bigger than the Beatles, richer than Croesus and duller than ditchwater, Jackson lives in a suburban house with his mother, father, two sisters and a pop-corn machine. Only rarely does he go completely over the top by plundering his wardrobe and gearing up in his favourite clothes – jeans and a T-shirt.

But he's done all right for himself.

4 Val Doonican

In an age of trendiness, Doonican has been a light in the darkness and a genuine dull hero who has dared to stand square against the whims and dictates of fad and fashion.

'I just sing the songs I like', he explains, 'rather than what is fashionable.' The result is that pop stars come and go but Doonican, with 23 TV series to his name so far, is forever.

His easy manner and gentle ballads have provided succour to dull music fans down the years, just as his rocking chair and cardigan have become essential dull accessories.

As for remaining ambitions, he says, 'I'd like to be a sort of Marks and Spencers of music.'

Apart from music, his passion is golf. 'Sometimes', he admits, 'I wish I had a bit more dynamism but at least with my temper I don't get in a panic about anything.'

5 Krystle Carrington

Even Dallas's Bobby Ewing is not half the wimp of *Dynasty's* Duchess of Dullness, Krystle Carrington – the dullest character on television today.

Krystle's true dullness lies in her ability to take every misfortune life hurls at her – miscarriages, divorces, car, riding and shooting accidents by the truckload – and to keep on smiling through: so unbearably nice, so unutterably dull. The murkier the intrigue and more dastardly the deeds of her co-stars the sweeter and duller she becomes.

When she launched her own perfume, 'Forever Krystle', the critical verdict was summed up by journalist, Sue Peart's view that, 'Forever Krystle is like its namesake, a bit too sweet, cloying and only to be applied in very small amounts. In fact, a little squirt among perfumes.'

Admits actress, Linda Evans, who plays Krystle with, as one critic put it, 'all the emotion of a goalpost', 'Krystle and I are very much alike. All I really want is a husband and child. Joan (Collins) adores the verbal confrontations, but it makes me sick every time I have to yell at her.'

6 Nick Owen

Living proof of Oscar Wilde's dictum that, 'Only dull men are bright at breakfast', TV AM presenter, Owen has been hailed as high priest and prophet of the Cult of Ordinariness.

Owen came forward and declared for dullness on first being made the station's front man: 'What I think I can bring to this station', he said, 'is ordinariness. Just a sort of normal ordinariness. I just want to be . . . er . . . ordinary.'

Since then, Owen's low-key style and relaxed wardrobe have banished the flashness of the Famous Five and at once banished the station's miserable ratings.

7 Fidel Castro

Not just a dreary dresser, Castro is also the world's dullest living public speaker, famous for his eight-hour speeches. Playwright, David Hare claims he won the Cuban revolutionary war merely by talking whole villages to death.

He is the dullest communist leader since Leonid Brezhnev, a recent biography of whom prompted Clive James to review:

'Here is a book so dull that a whirling dervish could read himself to sleep with it. If you were to recite a single page in the open air, birds would fall out of the sky and dogs drop dead.'

8 John Glenn

By his own admission a dull man, former astronaut and American presidential hopeful, Glenn used to dispatch his campaign staff in search of jokewriters to brighten up his act. From a white, Presbyterian, small-town, mid-west background, Glenn is all-American dull. He even married the dentist's daughter, his only girlfriend.

A great moment in dull history came when Glenn's spacecraft overheated dangerously on re-entry during the return leg of his famous flight as the first man to orbit the earth. While hipper astronauts might have 'freaked' or felt 'spaced out', Glenn's pulse rate rose by only one point, as he brought the craft safely through.

During his 1983–4 presidential campaign he even undershone rival Walter Mondale, himself said to have the charisma of a magnum of chloroform. Had he been elected, Glenn would have made the dullest US president since Jimmy Carter, of whom one commentator said, 'When Carter gave a presidential fireside chat, the fires went out.' And another, 'He couldn't hold his own attention.' Or even since Calvin Coolidge, of whom it was Dorothy Parker, of course, who asked, on hearing of his death, 'How can they tell?'

9 Bjoring Borg

Evidence of a possible biological basis to dullness came with the disclosure that Borg's pulse rate is barely half the human average. At any rate, the low-strung Swede didn't win five consecutive Wimbledons by being 'an amusing chap' or 'bags of fun', or yet another moaning Mac or bellyaching superbrat. He won by consistency, reliability and dullness when it counted, on the crucial points, while more flamboyant types were cracking across the net. By being, in short, a Volvo amongst tennis stars.

10 Peter Freedman

I don't think there was any one moment I first realized I was dull. But I do remember thinking how I was quite a swinger when I first started going to parties from two to five on Sunday afternoons instead of one to three. But then I remember noticing how the other kids had already started going to all-night sleep-overs and pre-teen discos. And then I suppose I knew.

By the time I got to adolescence, I was an unmistakably dull duck. Maybe I no longer nagged my parents to take me to the dentist as much. But while schoolfriends all wore red socks and campaigned against the uniform I relished wearing the identical drab grey suit day after day for five years.

I longed to be expelled for some outrageous prank to show at least I could go out with style. But while others were always pulling off wizard japes like blowing up the squash courts and knee-capping the geography teacher, dullness on it own was not an expellable offence.

I longed to be not just interesting but stylish, with-it and chic. I remember how I used to lock the door to my room at night and practise dunking a croissant in some Perrier as I had seen all the winebar designers and advertizing types do in the fashionable brasseries pictured in the glossy magazines.

But it never helped. Sure, I laughed at all the other guys' Barry Manilow jokes. But – though I've never admitted this before – I didn't understand them. Barry Manilow singing *Una Paloma Blanca* on *Sunday Night at the Palladium* was my idea of street cred.

Nowadays, I'm just as dull as ever. The difference is, I no longer worry about it. I'm not what you'd call a radical dull. I don't wear a

badge proclaiming, 'Dull is Fascinating'. I'm not even all that 'Glad to be Grey'. But rather simply glad of no longer being ashamed of not being all that interesting, chic, hip, with-it, stylish, sparkling and fascinating.

GREY MATTERS

'And What Do You Do?'
– A Guide to the Grey Economy

'People who do things exceed my endurance,
Oh, for a man who solicits insurance.'

DOROTHY PARKER

When it comes to jobs, dull folks know only two things for sure.

The first is that, *of course* it would be nice the next time they are invited (through some computer error) to the private view of an exhibition of kinetic sculpture at a Covent Garden gallery, and, just as they are beginning to wonder whether they've got B.O. or leprosy or something, who should materialize through the smog of Gauloises smoke but the sculptress herself, planting a kiss on both chics by way of bonjour and then, in a Parisian accent straight from Central Casting, asking, 'And zo, my liddle aubergine, what do you do?' . . . *of course* it would be nice to be able to answer:

'I'm a radical Zimbabwean poet, actually.' Or, 'I'm Senior Commissioning Editor, Actuality, at Channel Four.' Or even just, 'I write travel books.'

But the second thing they know is that, there may not be a heck of a lot of creative satisfaction in it, but *somebody's* got to do the job of sewing all those millions of little green alligators onto people's powder pink sports shirts.

And so, as much as they would like to reply, 'I'm Artistic Director and Prima Ballerina of Les Ballets Russes on our current world tour', they take strength from the knowledge and answer, 'Well, to tell the truth, I'm one of those people who sews . . .' But by the time they have got to 'little green alligators', even the drinks waiter has slunk back into the enveloping haze . . .

Jobs for the dulls

Dull folks in general then do the unglamorous but essential jobs that used to be known as 'work of national importance' – but which are now simply known as 'dull'.

They are all used, by now, to explaining to other people at parties:

'I'm Northern Area Sales Manager for a firm making posturepedic beds.'
'I'm Assistant Archivist (Fossils) at the Institute of Geological Sciences.'
'I'm a gravel and ballast contractor.'
'I'm with the Pru – an actuary, actually.'
'I do night-shifts in a pykelet-packing factory.'
'I'm a panty-hose crotch-closing machine operator.'
'I'm a fish technologist.'
'I'm with Sketchleys.'
'I scrape the burnt bits off sausage rolls in the canteen of the Commonwealth War Graves Commission.'
'I'm in sewage.'

. . . And are all used to having the other people react, 'Oh, how dull' and 'Oh gosh, that must be dull'.

There are certain areas, on the other hand, dull folks rarely go into. Few, for instance, have jobs which are 'International' or 'Creative'. Nor do you meet many dull designers or consultants. Scarcest of all are dull International Creative Design Consultants.

Among other jobs which few dull folks have are: rock journalist, fashion photographer, Mersey poet, performance artist, new wave film-maker or Style Editor of *The Face* magazine.

Some areas, though, are trickier. Scientists, for example, are known to be a dull bunch – unless, that is, they are mad or have recently won a Nobel Prize. And even then it's touch and go.

The point is, often the finest distinctions can make the difference. Compare, for example:

CHIC AND INTERESTING JOBS VS	DULL BUT ESSENTIAL ONES
War photographer	Photo-me-booth mechanic
Beat poet	Xmas card jingle writer
Formula One driver	Traffic warden
Astronaut	Planetarium cashier
Prima ballerina	Morris dancer
Travel writer	Reader's Digest book
Peking correspondent,	condenser
New York Times	Croydon correspondent,
Chat show host (London	*Croydon Advertiser*
Weekend Television)	Chat show host (hospital
Chef de Cuisine to a Russian	radio)
Grand Duke	Washer-upper, The Golden
	Egg

NOTE: To be an interesting person, it is important to have an interesting job. Important, but not essential, because many of the most interesting people don't have jobs at all.

They are known as 'freelance' – freelance wine bar designers, freelance human behavioural consultants, freelance travel writers.

Dull folks without jobs are known as 'unemployed'.

DULL EMPLOYMENT QUIZ
Q. Is it a crime to be a dentist?

The great and the dull – dull job heroes

– Physicist Albert Einstein for not only an undistinguished career as a patent clerk but for later claiming, 'If I had my life over again, I would have been a plumber.'
– Pop star Elton John for confessing, 'The best thing I can imagine for me is to have a record store and just serve behind the counter.'
– Nobel-winning playwright Tennessee Williams for his earlier career as a shoe salesman in St Louis, earning his crust fetching down deoderized insoles.
– Modern musical great, composer Charles Ives not only for sticking to his life-long career in insurance but for writing a standard work on the subject.
– Mountaineer and travel writer Chris Bonington for his initial vocation as a margarine salesman for Unilever.
– Novelist V.S. Naipaul for not only working as Press Officer of the Cement and Concrete Association but for being fired for lack of writing ability.
– Princess Anne for claiming that if she hadn't been a royal she would have been a lorry driver.
– Reclusive Swede Greta Garbo for her original career as a Stockholm soaplather girl and her later claim, 'I was never as proud as of my first week's wages.'
– Naturalist David Bellamy for his earlier career as a drain inspector.
– Symbolist painter Paul Gaugin for his true vocation as a stockbroker.
– Film star Sean Connery for formerly working both as a cement mixer and a coffin polisher.
– Renaissance superstar Leonardo da Vinci for being, of all things, an engineer.
– US Presidents Theodore Roosevelt, Harry Truman and Jimmy Carter for their true careers as respectively, cowpuncher, haberdasher and peanut farmer.
– US President Andrew Johnson, for pointing out in an 1843 speech that, after all, 'Adam, the father of the race, was a tailor by trade, for he sewed figleaves together for aprons. Cain was an artificer in brass and iron; Joseph, husband of Mary, mother of Jesus, was a carpenter by trade, and the probability is strong that our Saviour himself' – who presumably, could have had his pick – 'followed the same.'

Unsung heroes of dullness

LEAST CREATIVE WORK

Londoner Derek Wadlow specializes in tackling the dull and tedious jobs no one else will do.

Among his only slightly drear assignments have been: packaging 100 Victorian chamber pots, stringing and polishing 2,000 conkers for a conker championship and giftwrapping 1,400 coconuts.

But these were orgies of creative endeavour compared to:

* Counting how many T's there are in the Bible, for a firm running a competition to guess the number. 'It took 100 hours', he says. As to the final T total, 'I've forgotten'.
* Chopping half an inch off 300,000 matches, for a firm promoting a new metal container too small to hold existing matches.
* Packing 11,400 live earthworms into 1,900 polythene bags, for dispatch to students doing a correspondence biology course. 'I had trouble finding them in such numbers', he recalls, 'but eventually obtained them from a worm farm in Holland.'

LEAST DRAMATIC ACTING JOB

Compared to the great roles of English theatre, the début part landed by unemployed forklift truck driver, Michael Sutherton was nothing to go dancing topless in a fountain about. But a man has got to eat and a job is a job. Sutherton therefore was pleased enough to be picked from the dozens of hopefuls who auditioned for the role of the corpse in Tom Stoppard's play, *The Real Inspector Hound*.

Chosen for his lifelike portrayal of death, Sutherton said of his acting break, 'I have to lie still and look realistically dead for over an hour. It is just like being on the dole.'

MOST LONG-STANDING JOB

American, Curtis Reid earns his living standing still, doing nothing, for hours on end. He is a human mannequin, hired by shopping centres to stand on pavements and play dummy.

Though it may sound unexciting work it is not a job, he says, without its own hazards. Apart from the torches he has flashed in his eyes by people wanting to see if he is real, he has also had itching powder put down his back. 'And once someone stabbed me in the leg to prove that I was made of wood', he says.

He first got into standing still for a living after getting back from Vietnam. 'As part of my recuperation, I used to lie out in the sun', he explains. 'Suddenly, I would be shaken awake by someone wanting to see if I was OK. Without knowing it, I was slipping into a kind of trance.'

After perfecting his skills by standing still for a time in a local wildlife preserve, and training his heartbeat down to less than half its normal rate, a friend pushed him to try his first shopping centre.

'Even people who knew me thought that I was a mannequin. From then on I realized that this was what I wanted to do.'

DEVOTION BEYOND THE CALL OF DULLNESS

While flashier types flit from job to glamorous job, for ever larger salaries and faster cars, dull folks know how to stick things out.

How many Porsche-drivers or art students, for example, could match the dedication of such as:

* The sixteenth century's dullest mathematician, William Shanks, who spent twenty years of his working life calculating the value of Pi to 707 decimal places? (The fact that computers have since done it to eight million places in a few hours, and shown that Shanks, anyway, went wrong after the 527th place is not the point.)
* Or of equally dogged Frenchman, Christian Bouchardy, who has so far spent over ten years researching into otter droppings? 'I have collected more than 4,000 examples of droppings', he boasts, while confessing, 'but I have sighted only three otters.'
* Or of Britain's Hartwell Horne who put in seventeen years counting the number of verses, words and letters in the Bible to compile a table of Biblical trivia?
* Or of Bank of England man Abraham Newland who, in just sixty years of service, rose from junior clerk to chief cashier?

And who, for one twenty-five year spell from 1782, was able, through living in a suite above the bank as well, never to set foot outside the building.

And who, shortly before his death, wrote his own doleful epitaph:

> Beneath this stone old Abraham lies,
> Nobody laughs and nobody cries,
> Where he's gone and how he fares,
> No one knows and no one cares.

LEAST STARTLING WORK RESEARCH

Dull folks pride themselves on doing the unglossy but vital work that keeps society going.

That work doesn't have to be useful to be dull, however, was shown by Jon Haarberg and Rolf Norrman, the pair of Scandinavian researchers responsible for academia's first truly comprehensive study of the symbolic role of the cucumber in world literature.

Leaving no stone unturned and no cucumber unstudied in their epic investigation, the pair unearthed every reference to the vegetable back to 2,400 BC. They even threw in, for no extra charge and no conspicuous reason, a sub-study of the pumpkin.

Finally publishing the results of their probe in 1980 under the less than compelling title, *Nature and Language: A Semiotic Study of Cucurbits in World Literature*, Norrman and Haarberg were able to conclude, with what some might call staggering obviousness, that the cucumber's phallic shape had led it principally to be used as a symbol of fertility.

LEAST EXHILARATING WORK

New Yorker Lenny Dibari is a professional queuer. He waits in line for a living. 'I kind of enjoy it,' he says.

The British, for whom queuing is a sport, if not national pastime, may find it hard to understand the idea of someone being *paid* to stand in line. But in New York, where standing doing nothing is nearer to a sin, there is no shortage of those who find Dibari worth his wait in queues.

The people he meets at work often think he is mad, or else a follower of one of the more contemplative Eastern religions. Others take his number for future jobs.

He can and does tackle anything from post office queues to death certificate queues. But his speciality are the notorious lines at the New York State Department of Motor Vehicles.

Though not relentlessly exciting work, neither is it a job, he says, without its own dramas and adventures: the fights he sees, the queue jumping and the friends he makes.

Dibari, in fact, is just one of many professional queuers employed by the New York firm, Services Unlimited. Says its founder, David Alwadish, 'My mother wanted me to be a doctor, but I think I'm serving humanity in my own way.'

LEAST FASCINATING LECTURE

Too many people today, reckon dull folks, are trying to be too interesting. Good then to report for once on a case of people actively trying to be dull or, at least, boring.

Some, naturally, had to try harder than others when contestants gathered for Leeds University's first Golden Pillow Award for 'The Most Boring Lecturer of The Year' in 1974. Physicist and eventual winner, Dr Ashley Clarke, hardly needed to try at all.

Clarke beat off rival lectures on 'The Scunthorpe School of Ethno-Methodology' and 'German Vocabulary, With Particular Reference to Words for Parts of the Leg Below the Ankle' (winner of the Silver Pillow) with an exquisitely boring dissertation on 'Classical Mechanical Formalism for Motion in an Infinite Viscous Medium'.

'I was going to speak on "Classical *Hydraulic* Formalism for Motion in an Infinite Viscous Medium" but I didn't want to excite you all,' he quipped in introduction.

But after a slow start and stupefying middle, Clarke shifted into bottom gear to admit in conclusion, 'This all only applies in an *infinite* viscous medium so in practice it doesn't work.'

LEAST RIVETING TALK ON MANNED URINALS

But Ashley Clarke was made to seem a figure of Wildean wit by Leeds University French lecturer and two times Golden Pillow winner, Dr David Coward.

Coward bagged his first Pillow in 1976 with a numbing Marxist-Freudian analysis of a, by his own admission, 'not very funny' joke about coconuts.

But he really showed what he was made of the following year with an address of hallucinatory boringness on 'The Sociological Problem of the Manned Urinal'.

After some passionless waffle on the decline of personal service and a couple of weak lavatorial jokes, Coward was finally shouted off before even getting to his unique league table of manned urinals in inner city areas (in which Manchester ranked low).

Since retiring from competition after this second triumph, he has gone on to become a leading dull thinker. He theorizes, 'The stress on interest has been much to the detriment of education. Children should spend more time learning French verbs.'

Personally, he blames everything on the American Declaration of Independence. 'All that business about "the pursuit of happiness" –

what a dreadful word – creates false expectations. People's lives are bound to be disappointing after that.'

LEAST SUCCINCT PARLIAMENTARY SPEECH

One of the longest and least enthralling speeches of modern times was delivered in 1985 to a largely deserted House of Commons by Conservative MP for Burton-on-Trent, Ivan 'The Terribly Long-Winded' Laurence.

Rising to his feet at 5.12 a.m. on a crisp March morning late into an all-night sitting, Laurence addressed an amendment of the Government's seemingly innocuous Fluoridation Bill.

Came the dawn and he continued in full spate, hardly consulting the papers which lined almost one entire Commons bench as he sprayed statistics across the others.

Quoting sources ranging from the Superintendent of Waterworks at Wilmington, Massachussetts to the Newsletter of the Institute of Plumbers of Australia, the Burton MP ploughed on to 8 a.m. and the next landmark of his speech – the sounding of his watch alarm, followed by an explanation to his dwindling audience that it was now past his normal time for waking up.

Finally, at 9.35 a.m., as the sun climbed further into the Westminster sky, and having spoken longer in the Commons than any MP this century, Laurence rested his case.

Not, however, because he had run out of things to say – he had not – but merely because his oratorical skills were needed elsewhere: in the Old Bailey, as those of defending barrister in the country's record cash robbery. And so, assembling his papers, he exited the chamber in search of a no. 11 bus to work.

Asked afterwards whether any MPs had snoozed during what he regretted had been only a limited statement of the anti-fluoridation argument, Laurence confessed, 'People fall asleep during my short speeches sometimes, so I expect one or two did drop off towards the end.'

LEAST EXCITING DETECTIVE WORK

Dull folks know that not all of us can work making arts documentaries for London Weekend Television.

Some of us, like former nylon process worker, Sid Spencer must work as the world's first parish council 'Dog Dirt Lurker', patrolling the streets of West Hallam, Derbyshire, looking out for dogs in the act of contravening the bylaws, and reporting their owners.

'A Dog Dirt Lurker', explains councillor, Henry Shaw, 'hides behind bushes to see the offence.'

Spencer, sixty-four, got the job through an ad. in the *Ilkeston Advertiser* for a 'Bylaws Enforcement Officer'. Recalls council clerk, Peter Briggs, 'We were looking for someone who was fit, had an interest in the environment and an ability to communicate'. Spencer was chosen from a shortlist of candidates with these qualities.

'It was enjoyable', he says of the work. 'I was made redundant from my last job and it got me out of the house and occupied my time.'

On sighting an offence, he was to identify the culprit's owner either by approaching and asking their name or following them home.

But, he confesses, 'I never saw a dog offence. People in the village were very considerate with their dogs. And if they saw me coming they would go the other way.'

After three years without a prosecution the council was therefore forced in 1985 to re-examine the cost-efficiency of the service. Says clerk, Briggs, 'Now we have decided to put up notices instead.'

LEAST GLAMOROUS MEDICAL SPECIALTY

Compared to the glamour specialties of surgery or general medicine, Minnesotan doctor, Michael Levitt's field offers little glory. Dr Levitt has dedicated his working life to the study of intestinal gas. In turning medical attention to such neglected questions as the quantity of gas an average person passes and the reasons why stools float Dr Levitt has, however, earned himself a modest reputation as the physician who has 'given status to flatus and class to gas'.

MOST COMPLICATED GAS WORK

That the work of the dull need not always go unrecognized was shown in 1979 when President Brezhnev bestowed the Order of the October Revolution on his son, Yuri, 'for mastering the complexities of the Ohrenburg gas works'.

LEAST FASCINATING CIVIL SERVICE JOBS

Among the less conventionally exciting jobs listed in a recent booklet of Civil Service employment were, 'Senior Inseminator', 'Bees Officer (Seasonal)', 'Orbital Prosthetist' (a maker of glass eyes) and 'Object Cleaner'.

Dare to be Square –
'Le Style Dull' or Drab Chic

'Odds fish, Sir Percy, you're brainless, spineless and useless, but you do know clothes.'

THE SCARLET PIMPERNEL

'You've either got or you haven't got style*', sang Frank Sinatra.

Dull folks haven't got style. And aren't worried about it.

Dull is the ability to go out and spend £5,000 on couture clothes and toss them together so as to look like you picked them up for 50 pence at the local Oxfam. Except that no dull person would contemplate doing either.

Ultimately the dull feel the same way about clothes as they do about food – if they didn't have to, they wouldn't bother.

Dull folks may not have style, but they do have flare. At least in their trouser legs. And they do have taste. Lots of it. And all of it bad. Or so they're always being told.

Once, it was only art students and Continentals who had style. The rest of us had fashion, which we were either in, or in the case of dull folks, out of. Dullness was easy then. It was simply a case of wearing not so much last year's as last decade's fashion.

Thus, dull men were simply the ones ten years behind in the width of their ties or lapels. *Really* dull Victorians were the ones still wearing doublet and hose. (But dulls must guard against being so 'out' they're 'in' – against being met by the 'fifties look or the

---

* In that respect, point out dull thinkers, it is much like herpes, or a post office savings account – the first of which dull folks are less likely to have than the second.

'twenties look coming round the second time, when they're still wearing it the first.*)

But we are all art students – if not Artistic Directors – now. Or at least all expected to be. We all have to 'make statements' with our clothes. Statements in the case of dull folks, such as 'I am dull'. Or in the case of radical dulls, such as 'Dare to be Square' and 'Glad to be Grey'.

Which is not to say that dull folks know nothing about clothes. They are up with the great fashion debates of the day: questions such as 'Shall I wear a hat to church?' (naturally) and 'Would jeans be suitable for the theatre?' (never).

And they know a thing or two about style. They know, anyway,

---

* Dull folks don't go in for revival styles. They do not sport the Gatsby look or the Yanks look or the Chariots of Fairisle look. Nor plunder the racks of recycled chic in the overpriced emporia retailing American retread threads – the 'fifties look at 'nineties prices. Dull folks actually *lived* through the 'fifties – when Cliff Richard was 'a bit of a rebel' – and at the time, let them tell you, there was only one word for them: dull.

that if art students go out and buy mouldering, fifth-hand rags from street markets that this is known as 'Cheap Chic'. While if they choose to buy perfectly new clothes from nationally respected chain-stores, that this is known as 'Cheap Shit'.

It is in this society that dull folks are the ones for whom 'street fashion' means dressing like a traffic warden, a label is something you find on a Ketchup bottle, C & A is short for 'Chic and Arty' and Sebastian Coe is 'a bit of a dandy'.

Taking off the style

Dull dressing, above all, is about feeling comfortable and being yourself. Sincerity is the keynote.

Thus, dull men do not wear forties aviator jackets unless they fought in the Battle of Britain, berets unless they sell onions for a living, Doc Marten's unless they are skinheads or policemen, braces except to hold their trousers up or sleeveless Fairisle V-necks over white collarless shirts unless they are Paul McCartney (which they aren't) or auditioning for a Hovis commercial.

By the same token, dull women do not wear fake plastic jewellery unless their real plastic stuff is in being mended.

They don't wear sunglasses unless both the sun and they are out, in which case they prefer Boots plastic clip-ons over NHS hornrims to Porsche, Playboy, Wayfarer or Rayban mood shades.

Dull folks do not necessarily wear specially crumpled or torn clothes – and wouldn't, even if they could afford them.

When it comes to wearing other people's names on their clothes, dull folks are against it. Whose clothes are they anyway? they argue. Thus, they do not wear Gucci, Pucci, Fiorrucci, Gabicci or Cerruti. Or Gallini, Tachini, Martini, Cappuccini, Zuchini or Lasagna.

If their parents had wanted them to wear Yves Saint Laurent's initials on their ties, they presume they would have named them Yves Saint Laurent.

Which is why, when the whole world and its Y-fronts is plastered with designer labels, dull men are the ones wearing plain white cotton Y-fronts or old-fashioned boxer shorts. And not because they have just discovered them as part of the reaction against the reaction against paisley jockey shorts. But because they are *still* wearing them, and have always worn them.

And, of course, dull folks don't wear pinstripes unless they are commuters, which they so often are and hence so often do.

Putting on the warmth

After sincerity, comfort counts. As does warmth.

Thus, dull folks wear sensible footwear. Dull men wear Hush Puppies, galoshes, and corduroy slippers. Dull Chinawomen were the ones who refused to have their feet bound and insisted instead on Dr Scholl orthopaedic sandals.

As for warmth, dull women reckon, why spend six months' pay to shiver in a salmon-pink lace-satin Janet Reger negligée, when for a morning's you can have the snugness of real Thermolactyl against your skin in a long-sleeved Damart fancy-knit cosy top? Or the cosiness of a Scotcade Duvet-Wrap Snuggle-Up (the nearest a dull person can get to actually wearing a tea-cozy).

By the same token, who wants Schaparelli satin elbow-length opera gloves when for a snitch of the price you can insure against frostbite in nylon-lined Thermolactyl mittens?

Hence also, dull folks prefer Winceyette pyjamas to Oriental theme-satin kimonos, and would trade any number of sliver-thin Georgio Amani blazers for one good M & S anorak.

Drab don'ts

Beyond that, there are certain other rules.

Dull folks, for instance, do not 'Dress to Impress'. They dress to avoid being fired.

Dull folks do not wear shocking pink. They are the ones shocked. Neither do they wear red, orange or green socks, spectacles or hair. Hair, like clothes, is best worn grey. The little grey suit is a dull classic.

They don't wear fruit boots, zoot suits, brothelcreepers, winklepickers or Deely-Bobbers – and wouldn't, even if they knew what they were. Nor stovepipes, drainpipes (cause of water on the knee) or hosepipes.

They do not wear gold neck chains or radical rubberwear.

And dull folks don't overdress, except on the beach, where they still haven't got used to even men going topless.

Finally, dull folks do not say things like, 'If my Damarts could talk they would yawn.' But might be overheard requesting, 'Darling, do you mind if I go and slip into something more practical: an apron, say.'

DESIGNER ANIMALS

When it comes to animals on their clothes, dulls know the score. Though not before referring to the following chart:

CHIC ANIMALS FOR WEAR ON CLOTHES	DULL BUT PLUCKY ONES
Alligator	Dung fly
Coq (especially if Sportif)	Hedgehog (especially if
Polo pony	squashed)
Playboy bunny	Slug
Dolphin or Porpoise	Tapeworm
Fox	Tuna fish
Lobster	Maggot
Leopard (except on golf sweater)	Newt
	Sir Geoffrey Howe

Except that dull folks don't go in for animals on their clothes.

Drab do's – le style dull

What then *do* dull people wear?

Their dress sense centres on the style Drab Chic. (Also known as 'Le Style Dull' or 'Le Breakfast Television Look'.)

This involves wearing simple, unflashy clothes. The aim is to look like a BBC weather forecaster (Think: Michael Fish) or off-duty librarian; the ideal to be able to slip into an emergency meeting of the Soviet Politburo without being noticed.

Like some orthodox chicsters, drab chicsters like clothes that last.* Long enough anyway to achieve that special sheen on the elbows and trouser seat which art students assume they have spent hours of polishing to achieve.

But, finally, dull folks suit themselves.

---

* Old clothes worn by art students are known as 'Classic'. Old clothes worn by dull folks are known as 'Drab'.

The great and the dull – dull style heroes

– Actress Gilda Radner for confessing, 'I base most of my fashion taste on what doesn't itch.'

– Regency dandy Beau Brummel for riposting to a friend who had complimented him on his elegance at the races earlier that day, 'If you noticed me, I couldn't possibly have looked elegant.'

– Christian Dior Artistic Director Marc Bohan for asserting, 'It is ridiculous to criticize an official lady for looking dull. The only thing that matters is that she feels perfectly at ease and comfortable.'

– Actress and drab fetishist Linda Evans for coming out of the vast *Dynasty* closet and giving one in the eye to her overdressed co-stars by confessing, 'I'd love to have Krystle come on for once in her curlers and fuzzy old slippers'. And later adding, 'Sometimes when I'm doing one of those bedrooms scenes in some incredible peignoir worth £700 I'm dying for them to shoot me in a really old housecoat.'

– US president John Quincy Adams for allegedly wearing the same hat for ten years.

– King George V for wearing the same collar stud all his adult life.

– Labour leader Neil Kinnock for, according to wife Glenys, never going out without cleaning his shoes.

– Artist, poet and mystic William Blake, for being a famously drab dresser. 'Indoors,', wrote Victorian author, John Timbs, 'he was careful, for economy's sake, but not slovenly: his clothes were threadbare, and his grey trousers had worn black and shiny in front, like a mechanic's. Out of doors, he was more particular, so that his dress did not in the streets of London challenge attention either way.'

Unsung heroes of dullness

MOST TRUSTY NIGHT-SHIRT

When dull folks find a garment they can trust and feel comfortable in, they stick with it. As W.W. How of Ilford, Essex explained a few years ago in a letter to the *News Chronicle*:

'For 61 years I have worn a night-shirt. Recently, I decided to try pyjamas, but took the precaution to place my old friend within reach in case of failure. In one hour I was back in the night-shirt. We old-fashioned folk have difficulty in finding shops selling this trusty old-timed garment.'

MOST BELOVED WELLINGTON BOOTS

But W.W. How was a slave to fashion compared to retired farm labourer and dull hero Willie Radcliffe who showed loyalty beyond the call of dullness in 1983 by turning down the offer of a luxury, all-expenses paid, holiday-of-a-lifetime cruise to Hawaii because he was not prepared to be separated from his Wellington boots.

Explained Radcliffe, 'I don't think they would be the right thing to wear on a posh cruise and I couldn't wear anything else.'

NEATEST CLERICAL WORKER

In the matter of clothes, dull folks are practical. Few more so than the husband of a recent correspondent to *The People*. Explained the man's wife,

'My husband always sleeps with his tie on, knotted ready to slip under a clean shirt collar.

'He argues that the wear and tear by pulling and tugging to get his tie in place always wears it out long before its time.

'So once tied, it's very seldom undone. Fortunately, he's a clerical worker and doesn't get very dirty.'

LEAST REVEALING NEGLIGÉE

And then there is the problem the late Joyce Grenfell claimed was put to a friend of hers one day and without any preamble by the friend's cleaning lady. Confessed the latter,

'I don't like those chiffon nighties . . . they show your vest.'

LEAST TOPLESS BEACH

A young lady was lazing on the beach of that holiday playground of the genteel dull set, Frinton-on-Sea, one pleasant afternoon in 1929.

She was garbed in a bathing costume of what a *Daily Telegraph* correspondent of the day described as 'irreproachable modesty'.

The costume was held up by a single shoulder trap. And there was the rub. For as the council official who came over to confront her explained in sombre and reproachful tones, 'Frinton has always been a two-strap-town.'

MOST UNIFORM UNIFORMS

Dull folks do not wear army uniforms unless they are in the army, in which case they wear little else.

None less else than nineteenth-century French soldier, Marshal de Castellane, whose wardrobe comprised three identical uniforms, each bearing all his decorations.

The first uniform he wore by day. The second in bed at night. And the third . . . the third, we are informed, he reserved 'for bathing'.

LEAST SEXY UNDERGARMENT

'Socks are not generally seen as sexy in the bedroom', conceded the Sock Advisory Service in launching a recent promotion.

But, suggested the SAS, many women have secret fantasies about socks. It cited a Nottingham woman whose greatest turn-on was the sight of a man wearing just one sock.

'Socks can be sexy', said spokesman Oliver Sellers, 'They can be fun and exciting. When a man is standing his socks are unseen. As he sits down his socks are suddenly revealed.'

LEAST DEDICATED FOLLOWER OF FASHION

Eighteenth-century drab chicster Sir Harvey Elwes lived by the motto, 'Going to bed saves candlelight.'

When fashionable society came to visit it was greeted by Elwes always in the same attire – a drab full-dress suit beneath a decomposing greatcoat and shabby black hat worn low over the eyes.

And while fashionable society kept up with the styles of the moment, Elwes for his part never stooped to buying new clothes, relying instead when one garment finally went to rags on an ancestral clothes chest from which he would choose a mildewed replacement, frequently in the fashion of a century or more before.

LEAST TRENDY VICAR

No one ever accused Morgan Jones of being the type to wear something once and never again.

In fact, he wore the same shirt, coat and hat every day of the forty-three years he was vicar of Blewbury, Berkshire from 1781 to 1824. Every day, that is, apart from the four or five days a year on which he wore no shirt, to give it a chance to be washed. His coat and hat he never washed, to minimize wear.

Even in Jones's day, however, they didn't make clothes like they used to. And so, after just twenty-five years he found his hat, at least, was beginning to fray. Instead of blowing a year's collection money on modish new headgear Jones borrowed the hat worn by a local scarecrow. Or at least the hat's brim, which he deftly detached and fixed to the surviving crown of his own. Never mind it was quite the wrong colour. Nor that it wasn't quite good as new. It was good enough to see Jones through a further eighteen years.

His coat never needed such radical surgery, merely running repairs and the grafting of patches of lining and bits from the tail onto needier areas. His shirt got similar treatment until, just as the coat eventually became more of a jacket, the shirt underneath it grew too short to tuck in.

The drear gear awards for Britain's ten dullest dressers

Lack of style is the essence, the very juice (prune) of dullness.

True dullness is as timeless as fashion is fickle. Like style, you've either got it or you haven't.

Janet Street Porter, for instance, just hasn't got it, and never could, while Liberace is pure art student gone camping.

Some, of course, have got more of it then others. The ten folks who have most of it in Britain today are:

1 Michael Fish – as dull as the day is wet and the weather he reports on, Fish is not just the Sheikh of Drab Chic but an inspiration to dull men everywhere and a bulwark against the forces of trendiness assaulting even the former dull haven of TV weather forecasting.

The Fish wardrobe symbolizes all that is best about British forecasting. It is what gives both authority to his bulletins and credibility to the BBC's claim to be short of cash.

---

2 The Queen – the one woman in this country with the guts to wear horn-rimmed glasses with her crown.

3 Frank Bough – a gloriously uneccentric dresser. In an industry ravaged by the horrors of *Trendyosa Nervosa*, Bough has pioneered a new, more easy-going style and set the standard for breakfast TV presenters everywhere.

4 Sebastian Coe – L'Huomo Dull personified. Seb Coe in a C & A V-neck is like a square peg in a square hole.

5 Shirley Williams – High Priestess of le Style Dull à l'Anglaise and a Drab Chic heroine. No passive victim of drear group pressure, Williams discovered the crumpled look before it was fashionable and has stuck with it after.

6 Princess Anne – Past winner of Hollywood fashion designer, Earl Blackwell's coveted, DDT (Dull, Dreary, Tacky) Award.

7 Michael Foot – The human duffel bag. Few public figures have done more to promote a more informal, not to say, dishevelled style; or taken more stick for doing it: a Drab Chic martyr.

8 Val Doonican – Loose as a goose: 'Mr Relaxation' himself. The patron saint of cardigans.

9 Princess Margaret – Her Royal Drabness does her family proud.

10 John Selwyn Glummer – In the Conservative Party he may be rated quite a swinger but the rest of us see him in his true colours: light, medium and dark grey.

Eat, Drink and Be Dull –
Living off the Bland

'What in heaven's name is this?'
George V, on being served an avocado

Dull folks don't know much about food but they know at least that:

* Esau, who was no sucker, sold his birthright for a mess of potage – not for a mess of cold Andalusian gazpacho with four different types of croutons. And that:
* Jesus, who knew his way around, simply *multiplied* the loaves and fishes – he didn't turn them into fresh brioches and smoked salmon pâté. Or suggest the 5,000 might like to try the fish raw as this was *the* latest taste down the Bethlehem Brasserie. There would have been a riot.

Dull folks therefore are willing to risk public disgrace or forcible deportation by admitting that yes, they *like* the simple, no-nonsense food in trains, service stations, vending machines, hospitals, canteens, prison and The Golden Egg. And that no, they wouldn't rather starve than eat a Wendyburger or an Egg McMuffin. In fact, they had one for lunch.

But as with clothes, so with food – things for dulls have never really been the same since school: the golden age of semolina, tapioca and roly poly. Of rhubarb and custard, prunes and custard, spam and custard.

Beyond that, dull folks eat meat and two veg. Not, however, such high-rent, designer vegetables as aubergines, asparagus and artichokes. They stick to unflashy but digestible vegetables such as mashed swede, mushy peas and diced carrots. Or anything frozen or

55

tinned. Cold baked beans eaten straight from the tin are a dull delicacy.

Otherwise, they like their vegetables like their sweets: boiled. Anything less than an hour is raw.

The rule on salads is easy on the raspberry vinegar. Vinegar must be malt, salad cream Heinz and beetroots British.

They like their crisps plain, ice-cream vanilla and fruit stewed.

As for quiche, what's that? It simply hasn't reached their part of town.

Dull folks may not know the right way to peel a mango, or the name of all fifty-seven attachments to the latest Pastamatic De Luxe. But they do know all fifty-seven varieties of Heinz beans and the average frequency of every letter in a tin of alphabet soup.

Dull folks in general look back nostalgically to the days described by food writer, Jane Grigson, when, 'Basil was no more than the name of our bachelor uncles, "courgette" was printed in italics and few of us knew how to eat spaghetti or pick a globe of artichoke to pieces'. Many don't even have to look back – they are still living through them.

ONE THING DULL FOLKS NEVER EAT
Avocado-omelette filled croissants for brunch

GREAT DULL LINES FROM THE MOVIES
Burt Reynolds: 'Waiter, what is the soupe du jour?'
Dull but helpful waiter: 'It's the soup of the day, sir.'
The film *Paternity*

CORDON GRISE

Finally, however, dull stomachs live by four simple rules – the guiding principles of Cordon Grise (also known as 'Cuisine Dulle' or 'Le British Cooking')

1 There is no such thing as 'an overdone roast'.

2 The person who is tired of custard is tired of life.

3 (Out of respect to the millions of dull folks starving in France) Never eat in French what you can eat in English. Besides, it doesn't taste as good.

Thus, dull folks eat tinned peas but not *Petis Pois à la Français*, and fish and chips but not *Pommes Boulangères avec Loup de Mer Farci*, which is more like fish and chic.

(Are there dull Frenchmen, they wonder, who call their dessert 'Le Pudding'. Or simply ask the garçon for 'L'Afters'?)

4 If you're too good a cook you don't know who your real friends are.

Chez dulle, tres dulle

When it comes to eating out – which it rarely does for dulls – the first thing they want to know of a restaurant is not, 'Is it in the Michelin?', but, 'Do they take luncheon vouchers?'

Which is why you tend to find so few dull diners at places like Le Café Patisserie Créperie Brasserie des Artistes Bohèmes Parisiennes where, for barely more than the combined gross national products of Africa south of the Sahara, you can have the privilege of eating your bread roll straight off the tablecloth. And then having the head waiter come round afterwards to tell you how much he enjoyed your meal.

Other places you find very few dull diners are:
– Michael Caine's table at Langan's Brasserie (unless they are
Michael Caine, which they rarely are).
– The table next to the door in Sardi's (unless they are Dustin
Hoffman, or want a blast of sub-zero Manhattan smog in their
kisser – which they don't – every time some 'D' list celebrity
waddles in.)
– Restaurants where the chef has his name on the menu – unless
his name happens to be Berni, MacDonald, Colonel Sanders or
The Watford Gap Service Station Cafeteria.
– Or those where there *is* no menu but only an overtalkative waiter
interrupting to ask if he can 'tell you what's on tonight', before
launching into a singing menugram of foods you've never heard of
and wouldn't touch if you had. If they want a performance they'll
see a play – *The Mousetrap*, for example.

Dull folks finally, can be spotted in restaurants tasting the cold
Andalusian gazpacho with four different types of croutons before
pronouncing 'Mmmm . . . not bad, but needs more ketchup'.

ANOTHER THING DULL FOLKS DON'T EAT
Dull folks don't eat humble pie – any more.

Mine's a pineapple juice

Dull folks don't know much about drink but they know what they
like; and that it's not what they should.

Dull folks therefore can be spotted in Le Café Patisserie des
Artistes Bohèmes Parisiennes sending back the demi-tasse of
espresso with a twist of lemon for a Nescafe with condensed milk. Or
a plain old Robinson's Barley Water.

Or in Gault-Millau four toque restaurants turning away the
Chateau Lafite Rothschild 1858 because, as it's a special occasion,
they've decided to live it up and have *new* wine*.

Or else simply because they'd prefer a Diet Pepsi. And when this
arrives they do not sniff the ring-pull top before pronouncing, 'It's a
naive, domestic Cola, robust and yet diffident, impertinent while

---

* Dull folks are not all tee-totallers, though many do total tea: but Ty-Phoo rather
than Lapsang Souchong.

somehow compliant, with a maturity that belies its age and a versatility amounting to schizophrenia . . . Probably produced on the sunny side of the factory.' They just pour it and drink.

Dull folks do not all campaign for beer with more artifical additives and carbon dioxide. But neither do they trek days across country in search of improbably named 'real' ales that taste like old washing-up liquid, except without the flavour. In the CAMRA Pub of the Year, theirs is half a Barbican or a shandy and lemonade.

Dull folks are instinctively suspicious of places too slovenly to sweep up their sawdust and of drinks with too many things floating in them. If they want an umbrella in their drink, thanks, they'll stick in their own.

They therefore steer clear of overcute wineries full of graphic designers sipping Chablis or rich foreign students impressing au pair girls with exorbitant vintages.

And also avoid pink and green cocktail bars full of neon-lit palm trees and Simon le Bon lookalikes in overtight T-shirts.

They do not drink foreign liqueurs hawked in phoney French accents on out of focus TV commercials.

And they do not believe that Martini is 'the bright one, the right one', to be drunk 'any time, any place, anywhere'. The only place they would drink Martini is up a dark alley at knifepoint. And even then they would generally prefer a mug of Horlicks and a digestive biscuit.

THE JOY OF TAP WATER – THE ULTIMATE THIRST-QUENCHER

'Why buy bottled water at 40p a go, when you can get water from your tap free. . . . Don't be taken in by claims that bottled water is healthier, cleaner or in some way "better" for you. As far as we can tell, it isn't.' *Which Magazine*, 1982.

Dull folks agree. Why spurn nature's incredible gift, the ultimate thirst-quencher, in favour of eauver-priced designer water, pumped full of gas? Carbon dioxide is for beer not for water, which should be drunk as nature intended – straight from the tap.

Try it with ice. Or else on its own, au naturel. It goes with red meat and white, poultry and fish, Chinese and French – the perfect drink for every occasion.

DULL DRUGS

It is not true that dull folks can be found in the kitchen at parties trying to snort Pepsi. But it *is* generally true that, unless prescribed by their doctors, they tend to avoid drugs. In emergencies, however, they go by the following chart.

HIP DRUGS VS	DULL BUT HARMLESS ONES
Cocaine	Vic's Sinex (or Karvol Decongestant)
Pot	Syrup of Figs (or Pepto-Bismal)
Heroin and Cocaine 'Speedball'	Lemsip and Beecham's Powder cocktail
LSD	Andrew's Liver Salts (or Milk of
Glue	Magnesia)
	Sellotape

DULL DRINK QUIZ

Q. What happened to the dull woman when SHE discovered Smirnoff?

A. Sod all.

The great and the dull – dull food and drink heroes

– Post war minister and dull hero Clement Attlee for reputedly once asking the head pastry chef at the Savoy whether they had any, er, jelly?

– British football manager abroad, Terry Venables for asking, 'What do I miss about London?', and answering, 'The sausages. Not much else.'

– French chef Paul Bocuse for snorting, 'With this so-called nouvelle cuisine there is nothing on your plate and plenty on your bill.'

– First English head chef at the Ritz Michael Quinn for not only translating the menus into English and introducing rice pudding with raspberry jam, but also for confessing that while customers nibbled cordon bleu in the dining room he and his team could often be found wolfing beans on toast in the kitchen.

– Prime minister William Pitt the Younger for (one version of) his last words, 'I think I could eat one of Bellamy's pork pies.'

– Poet Percy Shelley for living entirely on currant buns.

– Poet Dylan Thomas for *subsisting* on pork pies.

– Labour leader Neil Kinnock and future king Prince Charles for their shared love of bread and butter pudding.

– Fashion designer to the glitterati Bruce Oldfield for his partialness to mushy peas, mashed potato and black pudding. And for confessing, 'I loved school dinners with all those wonderful stodgy puddings and semolina with jam. Another favourite is fish and chips: they remind me of summer holidays spent in Fleetwood, Lancashire.'

– Chinese emperor Hsuan-Chuang for, according to Frank Muir, banning the consumption of garlic inside the city limits.

– Rock star Ian Dury for pointing out, 'If Elvis Presley had eaten green vegetables, he'd still be alive today.'

– King Menelik of Ethiopia for eating a couple of pages of the scriptures whenever he felt poorly. And for finally biting the dust as well after pigging himself on the entire Book of Kings in an indigestible foreign edition.

– Labour Party founder and temperance activist James Keir Hardie for forbidding his MPs alcohol while in the House of Commons.

– Tennis star and dull heroine Sue Barker for admitting, 'I've only drunk once in my life. Never again. It was awful.'

– Writer F. Scott Fitzgerald for his habit of taking to his bed with a dozen cans of his favourite tipple Coca-Cola.

– St Brigid, Abbess of Kildare, for reputedly turning her old bathwater into beer (and thereby inventing real ale?) and serving it to visitors.

– A recent Bishop of Colchester for discreetly renaming his cat 'Shandy' after murmurings that its original name of 'Sherry' represented an undesirably strong intoxicant.

Unsung heroes of dullness

LEAST STYLISH HEIRESS

The world expects an heiress to live and die in a certain style. In Hetty Harland, New York heiress to a six million dollar fortune, the world was disappointed.

Harland eschewed such traditional staples as Beluga and pink champagne in favour of living entirely on cold porridge. And instead of downing her last bowl after a broken love affair or battle with consumption, she went the way of all flesh, aged eighty-one in 1916, after an argument over the cost of skimmed milk.

LEAST CHIC POPE

When still a young merchant living in Antwerp, Henvy VIII's future Lord Chamberlain and monastic hit-man Thomas Cromwell was approached by two Englishmen wanting his advice on the best way to lobby the Pope about the granting of two crucial pardons.

Knowing that the way to a Pope's heart is through his stomach and that this particular Pontiff was partial to a sweet dessert, Cromwell did not hesitate. He ordered the preparation of some English jelly and with it set off for Rome.

By telling the Vatican on his arrival that 'Kings and princes alone eat of this preserve in England' Cromwell wangled an audience. The Holy father, who presumably could have just said the word and had his choice of fresh lychees or mango and paw paw sorbets, instead agreed to try the jelly.

After trying a bit more, and then a bit more, he further agreed to grant the pardons. On only one condition – that Cromwell grant *him* the recipe for the scrumptious jelly.

MOST HONEST MENU TRANSLATION

Dull folks tell it like it is. They call a spade a spade and a carton of sweet and sour to go, a Chinese takeaway – not *Une Assiette de Pret À Manger à La Chinoise*.

One of the bluntest known examples of culinary plain-speaking was the menu translation offered by the Strand Palace Hotel one famously dull lunchtime in 1943. In French the menu read:

(a) *Ballotine de jambon Valentinoise*.

(b) *Assiette Froide et Salade*.

This, the management explained, in a commendably frank English rendering, stood for:

(a) Hot spam.

(b) Cold spam.

LEAST NOUVELLE CAFE MENU

The menu sighted by a *Daily Telegraph* reader in a cafe window near Basingstoke bus station, however, made the Strand Palace *carte* seem like nouvelle cuisine.

Among the delicacies offered were, 'Egg and Chips; Two Eggs and Chips; Egg, Bacon and Chips; Sausage and Chips; Two Sausages and Chips; Bacon, Sausage and Chips; Egg, Sausage and Chips; Egg, Two Sausages and Chips; Two Eggs, Sausage and Chips; Two Eggs, Two Sausages and Chips.' And this is not even to mention, 'Egg, Bacon, Sausage and Chips; Two Eggs, Bacon, Two Sausages and Chips; Egg, Bacon, Sausage, Beefburger and Chips . . .'

LEAST STYLISH SCHOOLMASTER

John Christie, the man who founded the Glyndebourne Festival Opera, was also a man noted for his prodigiously dull diet. He is said to have enjoyed his first career, of teaching at Eton, most of all for the food. Seven helpings of tapioca at lunch were nothing for Christie. When later in life he came to own his own restaurant the one item he insisted on seeing on the menu every day was milk pudding.

LEAST CHIC DELICACY

But Christie was playing in the mere foothills of dullness compared to Francis Henry Egerton, 8th Earl of Bridgewater and the Englishman who finally made the French pay for centuries of culinary oppression.

Egerton may have lived in Paris for thirty years from 1796 but he was never foolish enough to learn French, preferring to hold his dinner party conversation – on the few evenings he did not dine alone with his dogs – in Latin. But he struck his true blow for dullness by employing, at no small whack, the famous chef, Viard, whom he set to work at every opportunity cooking his favourite meal of boiled beef and potatoes and serving it to his French foodie friends as a great English delicacy.

LEAST FLASHY MIRACLE

One of the least ostentatious miracles of modern times was performed by the Reverend Richard Thomas, a member of the Catholic Charismatic Church and founder of the Lord's Ranch in New Mexico.

While flashier miracle workers heal the sick or bring back the dead, Father Thomas is better known for the more humble marvel of reportedly once turning fifty tins of condensed milk into 500 tins of the same.

LEAST ELEGANTE COOKING METHOD

Dull folks like their food boil-in-the-bag, heat-in-the-foil or thawed-in-the-microwave.

Only the quite inspirationally dull, however, will have even thought of trying their meals, as Englishwoman, Mrs Judy Boon, enjoys hers – steamed-in-the-dishwasher.

Her dishwasher specialty is trout. 'I get large trout from a fish farm', she explains, 'and slot them into the place for cups on the top rack.' Square trout, she advises, fit better than long ones.

She then merely sets the machine on to the plate-washing cycle. 'And in 50 minutes the trout are perfectly cooked.'

LEAST DISTINGUISHED VINTAGE

L'Eau Duponde never pretended to be one of the great vintages. The restaurant of Malcolm Moyer's Ruddy Duck pub near Peakirk, Northants listed it thus: 'Matured locally. A heady wine, varying in colour with unique bouquet. It should be drunk with a pinch of salt.'

Demand for the wine was such, however, that Moyer was eventually forced to take it off his list. By then over fifty customers had ordered it in three months. 'But I always said it was out of stock and suggested an alternative', he recalls.

He even remembers one man explaining to his girlfriend that L'Eau Duponde was an excellent wine he had seen before in London. 'Sometimes', Moyer admits, 'it was hard to keep a straight face'.

Hard also, presumably, not to let on that L'Eau Duponde – or, in English, (Duck) Pond Water – was merely Moyer's revenge on the wine snobs who droned on in his restaurant.

LEAST WORRYING DRINK PROBLEM

Yet another way the dull are disadvantaged was pointed out a few years ago by a correspondent to the *Daily Mirror*.

'There are many songs in praise of beer and wine. Teetotallers like myself would appreciate songs for lemonade and other fine soft drinks. It would add to the enjoyment of gay teetotal parties.'

THE WORLD'S DULLEST FOOD

Which is the dullest food of them all? Stewed prunes have their adherents. There are those who speak highly of porridge, particularly served warm and without sugar or milk. But for *Daily Mirror* columnist, William Connor, there was only one contender:

'Boiled cabbage *à l'Anglaise*' he reckoned, 'is something compared with which steamed coarse newsprint bought from bankrupt Finnish salvage dealers and heated over smoky oil stoves is an exquisite delicacy. Boiled British cabbage is something lower than ex-Army blankets stolen by dispossessed Goanese doss-housekeepers who used them to cover busted-down hen houses in the slum district of Karachi, found them useless, threw them in anger into the Indus, where they were recovered by convicted beachcombers with grappling irons, who cut them in strips with shears and stewed them in sheep-dip before they were sold to dying beggars. Boiled cabbage!'

Which is all a bit hard, considering that many dull folks happen to like boiled cabbage.

Overland to Thornton Clevelys – Dull Travel and Adventure

'I would rather have the money as I am booked to go to Cleethorpes.'

Yorkshirewoman, Heather Dillon, on hearing she had won a dream holiday-of-a-lifetime for two to Bangkok.

Once it was only the upper classes who Travelled – on their interminable Grand Tours and Voyages Philosophiques. Plus the odd mad-cap explorer, footloose Victorian lady or show-off travel writer.

But we are all travel writers now. Or at least all expected to be. All expected to seek out foreign adventures and needless dangers in faraway places of which we were once proud to know little and care less.

Call them unadventurous if you like then but dull folks believe the point of a holiday is to relax and unwind, not to:

* Lay out a year's income to visit some overcrowded Chinese resort where you can't sleep nights for the clatter of travel writers bashing out their next volume on *The Undiscovered East*.
* Cram into a Land Rover full of alcoholic Australians outward bound for some godforsaken desert where the one road is jammed with trans-global explorers and overland trekkers competing to see who can come home with the most incurable tropical disease. (Dull folks are not the type who only feel what they're doing is Real Travel when at least three members of their group have been kidnapped by the local guerilla faction and the rest shot as suspected drug smugglers.)
* Risk their lives going free-fall parasailing or shooting the Victoria Falls in a chamber pot – too scared to scream but too scared to admit they'd rather be home with a cup of Bovril and a good book.

Dull folks therefore do not talk in loud voices at parties about the time they saw the migration of the white rhino, went conga-wrestling off the Great Barrier Reef and skinny-dipping in the Lake of Heavenly Peace, pedaloed single-handed across the Pacific, shot the last silver-backed gorilla on the banks of the Okavango and washed their dentures in the source of the Orinoco – and wouldn't, even if they had done these things.

Dull folks, anyway, tend to find a fortnight away from the office simply isn't long enough to retrace Alexander the Great's conquest route through Asia Minor and the Levant, motorbike solo from Cairo to the Cape, or mount a realistic expedition in search of the lost world of Atlantis.

By the same token, dull folks are not inclined to spend their entire holidays in quest of undiscovered Greek islands (if they're so terrific, why are they still undiscovered?) on which to spend all day tracking twelve miles up the coast in search of a deserted beach.

But neither do they deliberately seek out crowds. They therefore, on the other hand, do not go to Paris in the springtime, Cannes for the film festival, Venice (before it finally sinks under the weight of travel writers and documentary crews) for the Biennale, Oberammergau for the Passion Play, Rio for the carnival, Florence for the galleries, Sorrento for the sunset or Peking for love nor money.

Dull folks do not necessarily get jetlag every time they put the clocks back or spend every holiday eating paella and chips in Mallorca. But yes, they do know what a package is and no, they don't see the appeal of three weeks in a leaky farmhouse in the Dordogne in order to come back with a raintan, looking like a prune.

Where then do dulls go?

Dull folks like to holiday in countries like . . . well, like England and like Wales. Unexotic but democratic countries with reliable plumbing and up-to-date cricket scores.

(Ireland is a bit far and anyway, dull folks feel rather threatened by the Irish Tourist Board ads proclaiming that 'The Most Interesting People Go to Ireland'.)

They stay in Britain, however, not because 'We're hardly in the country the rest of the year' or because they've been everywhere else but because they don't have a passport or simply because they prefer the food.

GREAT HOLIDAYS AND JOURNEYS VS DULL BUT RELAXING ONES
OF THE WORLD

White-water rafting down the Bio Bio river in Chile	Pedaloing across the municipal reservoir in Thornton Clevelys
A short walk in the Hindu Kush	A long walk on Southend pier
A month in the Kashoggi Suite of the Cipriani Hotel, Venice	A week in a luxury villa-van in the St Ives Bay chalet and caravan park
Summer in a friend's castle in Yorkshire or villa in Tuscany	A long-weekend in a self-catering bungalow in Ilfracombe
Ice-walking on Alaska's Great Glacier Bay	Hill-walking in the Cotswolds
Club Med, Paradise Island	Club Pontinental, Douglas, Isle of Man
The Golden Road to Far Cathay	The A35 to Bournemouth
By camel train across the High Atlas mountains	By Southern Region across the South Downs
By slow boat to China	By cross-channel ferry to Ostend
By Orient Express to Constantinople	By National Express Bargain-breakaway to Bude

---

The great and the dull – dull travel heroes

– Traveller Freya Stark for being asked, 'Does travel broaden the mind?', and answering, 'No'.
– King George V for contending, 'Abroad is awful. I know because I've been there.' And
– King George VI for agreeing, 'Abroad is bloody.'

69

– The Fifth Earl of Cardigan for advising, 'Never go abroad. It's a dreadful place.'

– Writer, Daniel Defoe for knocking off the seminal travel book, *A New Voyage Round the World* without leaving his desk in London.

– Novelist and poet Victor Hugo for capturing the Gallic spirit of adventure and daring-do with the observation, 'Everything that exists elsewhere, exists also in Paris.'

– Such traitors to their profession as travel writer Paul Theroux for confessing that, '50 per cent of travel is direly boring.'

– And travel writer Hugo Williams for explaining that, 'The word "travel" is the same as the word "travail", meaning labour. It comes from the Latin trepalium, an instrument of torture involving three wooden stakes.'

– Boxer Brian London for being asked by American reporters what he thought of L.A. and answering, 'It's all right but it couldn't hold a candle to Blackpool.'

– Actor Richard Briers for confessing, 'I live quite a boring life. . . . I was born in Wimbledon fifty years ago. Now I live in Chiswick. I have only travelled seven miles in half a century'.

– Painter Benjamin Robert Haydon for being the one person to notice that, 'Paris is a filthy hole'.

– Former Australian First Lady Siona McMahon for remarking of the native women she met on a state visit to China, 'I thought it was a great pity they were not taught to look after themselves and have their hair done nicely.'

– Playboy and suspected Porsche-driver Mark Thatcher for showing the dull in every man by getting lost crossing the Sahara.

– Greek philosopher Socrates for contending, 'See one promontory, one mountain, one sea, one river and see all.'

– The authors of the Chinese book of wisdom, the *Tao te Ching*, for summing it up,

> Without going out of the door,
> One can know the whole world,
> The further one travels,
> The less one knows.

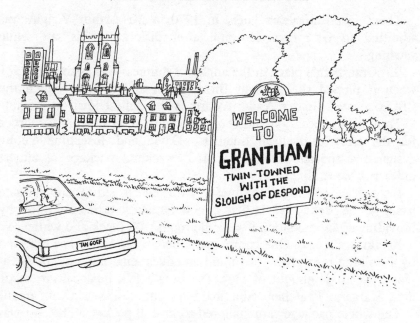

The seven wonders of the dull world

1 THE WORLD'S DULLEST TOWN

It has been said that the most exciting thing ever to come out of Grantham – widely rated as the world's dullest town – is the A1. To those, however, who further say that nothing of interest has happened in this sleepy market hamlet since the 'fifties (the 1650s, that is, when Isaac Newton passed through briefly) Granthamites point out that as recently as 1963 the town council took the uncharacteristically bold step of erasing the words, 'Men's Lavatory' from a glass door in preparation for a visit by the Queen Mother.

In what was to prove an eventful year for the town, the lady mayoress then went on in a controversial speech to take a stand against the rising tide of bareheadedness among local women. 'A new hat', she quipped unambiguously, 'does a woman a world of good. It brightens her whole outlook.'

Grantham's reputation was further enhanced in 1966 when road safety experts identified it as a major drivers' 'fatigue spot'. The large number of accidents recorded on the Grantham stretch of the Great North Road was attributed to the fact the town appeared to be the point where drivers northbound from London seemed suddenly to tire.

71

Then, just four years later, in 1970, a Mr Arthur Wright was admitted to Grantham Hospital after dislocating his jaw while yawning.

But Grantham's place in the annals of dullness was assured in 1981 when it pipped the likes of Birmingham and Slough to win the BBC's coveted Golden Yawn Award as the dullest town in Britain.

To mark the occasion and confirm Grantham as the holiday mecca for the truly dull, local hoteliers, David and Josephine Young designed a special 'Bed and Bored' weekend package of almost indescribable drabness.

Instead of intimidating guests with lavish suites and private jacuzzis, the package gave them a more authentic taste of local life by providing accommodation in a single room with black and white TV.

Breakfast on Day One comprised a boiled egg. This was followed by a walking tour of the town and an educational talk on The Great North Road. Highlight of Day Two was a talk on local girl made dull, Margaret Thatcher and a final blow-out of dinner in your room.

The whole package came tailored to fit dull pockets. The cost was £20 for Day One, £15 for Day Two, with the Youngs offering a pound to anyone who stayed a third night.

2 THE WORLD'S DULLEST COUNTRY

As far as dull folks are concerned, Switzerland is more than just the country which lays claims to the world's earliest known set of upper and lower dentures. More, even, than travel writer, Jonathon Raban's 'country of phobic handwashers living in a giant Barclays Bank'.

It is also Europe's dull heartland and the summer playground of the international dull set (Margaret Thatcher is just one of the VIDs (Very Important Dulls) who holidays there annually.)

Traveller, Henry Lord Brougham found Switzerland, 'A country to be in for two hours, or two hours and a half, if the weather is fine, and no longer. Ennui comes in the third hour and suicide attacks you before night.'

But it was Orson Welles who captured the spirit of the place in the film, *The Third Man*. 'In Italy', he said, 'for 30 years they had warfare, terror, murder, bloodshed but they produced Michelangelo, Leonardo da Vinci and the Renaissance. In Switzerland they had brotherly love, they had 500 years of democracy and peace, and what did they produce? – the cuckoo clock.'

Too-clever-by-half-wit, Oscar Wilde, however, rated it equally drear, remarking, 'I don't like Switzerland: it has produced nothing but theologians and waiters.'

Which is all rather unfair to Switzerland, considering that it has also produced the numbered bank account, Valium and Ovaltine; and that dull folks happen to like Ovaltine.

3 THE WORLD'S DULLEST CITY
'Imagine', wrote critic, James Agate, 'Birmingham encircled with a ring of Streatham-like suburbs and set down in the middle of Surrey' – and you have the world's dullest city: Philadelphia.

4 THE WORLD'S DULLEST TOURIST ATTRACTION
The world's dullest tourist attraction is a sock. Not just any old sock, but a particularly old and especially baggy one.

It is known as 'The Yorkshire Sock' having been deposited in the boggy Yorkshire soil by an untidy Viking a thousand years ago.

The sock was recently given its first wash in more than a millenium by museum official, Jean Glover, before being mounted and set on display in York's popular Viking Centre.

Said Ms Glover of the sock, 'It has excited worldwide interest. Now it will become a major tourist attraction.'

5 THE WORLD'S DULLEST TOURIST RESORT
Dull folks are not the type who need to travel 5,000 miles and be attacked by an undiscovered tribe of dart-blowing cannibals in order to feel they have properly been on holiday.

Even so, when Bradford council first announced plans for a programme of attracting tourists to the town, not everyone, admits tourism officer, Maria Glott, was convinced by the idea. 'Local folks found it difficult to imagine why anyone should actually want to come to the area; they didn't believe it had anything to offer.'

But the fact is, there is more to Bradford than dark satanic mills – derelict warehouses for example, as well as disused railway sidings and the least visited cathedral in Britain. The combination, allied to shrewd targeting of the dull market, has already made Bradford the holiday boomtown of West Yorkshire.

'Bradford Metropolitan District – a surprising place', is the less than magical title of the brochure the council puts out to entice visitors. Most of whom have so far come on package weekends, with highlights including visits to Yorkshire's oldest pork pie shop, the largest collection of walking sticks in the world, some old wool warehouses and Bradford's answer to the Venice-Simplon Orient Express, the popular Middleton colliery railway.

But the single attraction that merits a visit to Bradford on its own for any truly dull tourist is the opportunity to tour a local factory and see how thermal underwear is made.

6   THE WORLD'S DULLEST PLACE NAME

The world's dullest place name is GREAT SNORING, a village in Norfolk.

7   THE WORLD'S DULLEST NATIONALITY

Switzerland may be the world's least exciting country. But can there be a nationality duller than the English? The Swedes may make safer cars, the Norwegians stolider drama and the New Zealanders more tranquilizing travelogues. But for all-round, rock-ribbed, copper-bottomed dullness who is there even to enter the ring with the nationality that invented cricket, Birmingham, English food, the tune to God Save Our Gracious Queen and the long-sleeved Damart Thermolactyl Fancy-Knit Cosy-Top?

It was Anthony Trollope who reckoned that two Englishmen meeting in the desert would not speak unless introduced, and George Mikes who noticed that while Continentals have sex, the English have hot water bottles. But it is the Irish who tell jokes about the dullness of the English.

Yet dullness is a national strength, the foundation of our democracy, the thing that got us through the war under the maxim of 'business as usual'. It is one of the things we do best, and of which we ought to be proudest.

We are at heart a nation of shop-keepers and Clement Attlees – at risk of becoming a nation of coke-fried rock producers and Porsche-driving wine-bar designers, unless more of us stand up and join the fight for the right to be dull.

DULLEST COMMENT AT THE GREAT WALL OF CHINA

Dull folks know that building the Great Wall of China was not one long creative ideas session. They therefore do not insult the memory of the millions of dull workers who toiled on its construction by making glib quips when visiting.

The dullest recorded remark on visiting the Great Wall of China, however, was made by President Richard Nixon. Instead of showing off to the press corps by attempting some wiseacre crack likely to earn a place in the quote books but sure to flummox the interpreter and embarrass the Chinese leadership in the process, Nixon showed his statesmanship by casting a glance down the length of the wall, pulling himself up to his full height, fixing the Chinese delegation square in the eye and, speaking for one nation unto another, declaring . . . 'It's a great wall'.

Equally unmomentous remarks on momentous occasions were those by:

* Yuichiro Miura, 'the man who skied down Everest', and who, after notching speeds of 150 k.p.h. and nearly killing himself in the process, dared to suggest, 'The end of one thing is the beginning of another.'

* Explorer Henry Morton Stanley who hacked his way through 500 miles of African jungle to deliver the line, 'Dr Livingstone, I presume.'

* The Queen who, on first sighting Niagara Falls, had the boldness to observe, 'It looks very damp.'

Grey areas – the ten dullest towns in Britain

Dull folks know that there is room for only so many of us in Chelsea or Notting Hill Gate.

The rest of us must live out in the semi-detached suburbs and dull heartlands, down on the unfashionable pages of the London A–Z and unchic map numbers of the Reader's Digest Book of the Road.

Research shows that the greatest densities of dull population are concentrated in the following 10 'Grey Areas'.

1 Grantham – centre of the dull world; where the dull go when they die.
2 Birmingham – As English Tourist Board Chairman, Michael Montague put it, 'Very few overseas visitors are quite sure where Birmingham is'.
3 Aberystwyth – 'The perfect town for the unambitious man', judged Wynford-Vaughan Thomas. Dull capital of Wales.
4 Basingstoke – our kind of town, Basingstoke is. As John Arlott phrased it,

> Of Basingstoke in Hampshire,
> The claims to fame are small,
> A derelict canal,
> And a green and cream Town Hall.

5 Chelmsford – nominated by Charles Dickens: 'If anyone were to ask me what in my opinion was the dullest and most stupid spot on the face of the Earth, I should decidedly say Chelmsford.'
6 Tunbridge Wells – Was it Harold Wilson who said, 'A week is a long time in Tunbridge Wells'? So is an hour. One of those places that before you die you promise yourself you'll never go.
7 Hull – 'How dull is Hull', felt Peter Freedman. Visit the docks for a taste of the local colour – grey.
8 Edinburgh – Playwright, Tom Stoppard's 'Reychyavik of the south', where, apart from the aberration of the Festival, the favoured pastime is still sitting around in coffee bars sighing heavily into one's coffee.
9 Eastbourne – 'The extreme quiet and absence of the ordinary gaieties of watering places are among the more obvious characteristics of Eastbourne', advised the Victorian guide-book, *Where Shall We Go?*, i.e. Bournemouth but without the nightlife.
10 Guildford – a hotbed of social rest; the Switzerland of Britain.

Dull Folks 'Do It' in Bed –
Dull Sex and Romance

'Listen, Bond, it'd take more than crabmeat ravigote
to get me into bed.'
Jill St John to Sean Connery in *Diamonds Are Forever*

Dull folks are not into the 'New Celibacy'. They are still into the old celibacy.

Call them old-fashioned if you want, but dull folks still do things like 'go steady' and 'get married'.

Thus, dull women are not cheap. Which is not to say they are expensive. Merely that they don't believe in 'doing it' (holding hands) the first time they go out with a man.

Dull folks may not know their G-Spot from their F-Plan. They may think that Herpes is the name of an aircraft carrier and the Kama Sutra an Indian restaurant.*

But they know at least that Romeo, who was no slouch in the romance stakes, was not given to interrupting Juliet at her moment of heavenly transport to tell her to hold everything while he flicked to page 638 of *Yet More Joy of Sex* and checked where the elbows went in the Mexican Whirligig. Or while he adjusted the wide-angle focus on the bedside video camera.

Dull folks, in short, are not up with all the latest erogenous zones, sexual gadgetry and tortuous positions devised by oversexed foreigners with suppler bodies and dirtier minds.

Thus, Porsche-drivers have water beds (often in the back seat). Dull folks (who, anyway, get seasick) have hot water bottles – the only sexual aid they know.

Dull folks, furthermore, do not take out personal ads in smart weeklies to the effect that, 'Successful, attractive, intelligent, slim, dynamic, high-flying, interesting, sparkling, witty and fascinating international creative design consultant with 300 foot yacht and

77

private island in the Caribbean seeks similar to share relationship and futon.'

But they might own up to a Valentine's Day two-liner to the effect that 'Tiger Humphlekins Wants to Snuggle Baby Womble'.

Dull women do not dream of marrying a millionaire. They dream of marrying someone with a paid-up Access card.

Hipper dulls can be found at risqué suburban parties tossing their car keys into a pile on the floor and then swapping Volvos for the weekend.

Perverts go in for S & M. Dull folks stick to M & S.

GREAT DULL ADMISSIONS

'I don't know how to kiss or I would kiss you.
Where do the noses go?'
Ingrid Bergman to Gary Cooper in *For Whom the Bell Tolls*

Places dull folks don't long to have sex

Dull folks are modest. They are also discreet. And often romantic. They therefore do not have any particular longing to have sex:

– On a chairlift in St Moritz or cable car roof in Gstaad.
– On the boardroom table of an international creative design consultancy during a board meeting.
– On the backseat waterbed of a nail-lacquer red Porsche turbo.
– On a fireside tiger-skin.
– In the unisex WC of the Chase Manhattan bank in Paris.
– In the first-class lavatory of a 747 into New York (unless they want a slipped disc or hiatus hernia, which they don't).

If God had intended us to fornicate in a cramped toilet at 30,000 feet, reckon dulls, he wouldn't have given us bedrooms.

GREAT DULL PICK-UP LINES
'Your eyes are the colour of our dog's'.
Adrian Mole, aged 13 ¾ to Pandora Braithwaite

Quiz: Are you the dull lover

1 Which of the following do you most frown on:
a. Sex before marriage?
b. Sex before breakfast?
c. Sex before *Match of the Day*?

2 Would you say that oral sex is:
a. What happens during a dirty phone call?
b. The cause of oral contraception?
c. Talking your way out of it?

3 It's spring time. Love is in the air. You've met someone new. You decide on a romantic weekend away: two days of fantasy, passion and bliss. Do you head for:
a. Paris?
b. Venice?
c. Bournemouth?

FOR WOMEN ONLY

4 Do you call the person you live with your:
a. 'Lover'?
b. 'Significant Other' or 'Meaningful Associate'?
c. 'Husband'? or 'Wife'

5 Prince Charming shows in town, promising to hitch up with whoever fits his glass slipper. You:
a. Hope for his sake it's not your uncle Basil?
b. Think how handsome he is and squeal with delight?
c. Think, 'Just what I need, a foot fetishist'?

FOR MEN ONLY

6 The food was good, the lights are low, the mood is right. *Le moment just* has arrived. You:
a. Softly caress her silken thigh and whisper sweet nothings into her ear?
b. Sense she is inching towards you and quickly ask, 'Are you *sure* you wouldn't like another cup of coffee?'
c. Think, 'What the heck, there's nothing on TV'?

Now check your scores:
```
1 (a)  1 (b) 3 (c)  4
2 (a)  1 (b) 2 (c)  5
3 (a)  0 (b) 0 (c)  5
4 (a)  0 (b) 0 (c)  5
5 (a)  2 (b) 0 (c)  5
6 (a)  0 (b) 4 (c)  3
```

How did you do?.

0–5   Self-confessed art student.
6–10   Probable Porsche-driver.
11–15   Sensible though no Queen Victoria.
16–25   You dull devil.
26–30   Dull is not the word.

---

*DULL BUT TRUE FOOTNOTE Smirnoff Vodka was forced to abandon its famous ad-line, 'I thought the Kama Sutra was an Indian restaurant until I discovered Smirnoff', when consumer research found that 60 per cent of the public *did* think it was an Indian restaurant.

The great and the dull – dull sex heroes

– Novelist Graham Greene for being asked in a school question-naire, 'What do you admire most in a woman?' and answering, 'Cleanliness'.

– Royal spouse and female half of the 'Romance of the Century', Wallis Simpson for confessing, 'I have had two husbands and I never went to bed with either of them.'

– Woman about town Bianca Jagger for admitting, 'Unless there's some emotional tie I'd rather play tennis'.

– Popster Boy George for declaring, 'I don't miss having a sex life. I'd rather have a cup of tea.' And later adding, 'Bi-sexuality . . . it's so art school.'

– Former First Lady Jackie Onassis for, according to Gore Vidal, reckoning that sex was a bad thing because it rumpled the clothes.

– Starlet Brooke Shields for asking, 'What does "good in bed" mean to me?', and answering, 'When I'm sick and stay home from school propped up lots of pillows watching TV and my mum brings me soup – that's good in bed.'

– Founder of British family planning, Marie Stopes, for remaining a virgin until age thirty-six, including throughout a five-year marriage.

– Emperor Napoleon for coining the dull motto, 'Not tonight Josephine'.

– Italian superstud Casanova for confessing in his memoirs that he was impotent by the age of forty. And that, 'Without love this great business is a vile thing.'

– Novelist D.H. Lawrence for, despite all his dirty books, being an utter prude, unable to tolerate lewdness from others, or contemplate, let alone indulge in, lovemaking in anything but complete darkness. 'The messiah of sex', author Carol Dunlap has written, 'was happiest when peeling potatoes or scrubbing floors.'

Unsung heroes of dullness

LEAST SHOWY GESTURE OF LOVE

Greater love have few men than that they should do for their wife what the husband of a correspondent to the *Daily Mirror* did nightly for his. 'My husband is thoughtful', explained his spouse. 'Our hot water bottle has started to leak, and I can't stand to get into a cold bed. So every night my husband plugs in the electric iron. While I am undressing he irons my side of the bed. Then I get in and iron his side.'

LEAST SCINTILLATING LOVE LETTER

The least riveting love letter ever written was sent by nineteenth-century painter, Marcel de Leclure to his loving turtledove, Magdalene de Villatore. The letter began promisingly enough with the words, 'Je vous aime'. Reading on, however, de Villatore found that the next three words were also 'je vous aime'. As were the next 5,624,991.

Instead of writing out the lovesome phrase all 1,875,000 times – a thousand times for each year of the date – himself, Leclure was shrewd enough to hire a clerk for the job. But instead of just telling the man to dash off the key sentiment 1,875,000 times, as a more impersonal lover might have done, Leclure was besotted enough and dull enough to stand over him and dictate the entire epistle word by word. And, in case the scribe misheard at any point, the lovesick painter had him repeat his exact words after each 'je vous aime'.

THE NEXT LEAST SCINTILLATING LOVE LETTER

The 700 love letters sent to a Midlands girl by a Taiwanese admirer, however, cannot have been hugely more enthralling. At least not to their recipient. She married the postman who delivered them.

LEAST PASSIONATE LOVE-MATCH

That it is not only *possible* for a marriage to be both dull and happy but that the two tend naturally to go together was shown once more by one of the least ardent love-matches of recent times, described a few years ago in a letter to *The Daily Herald*.

'I fell in love with my husband', explained its author, 'simply because he was so different from every other boy I have ever met. He did not like love-making and neither did I. He has never actually

told me he loves me.

'Now, after 26 years of marriage, I sometimes wonder if I have missed something, but I am happy. He is a wonderful husband.

'He never actually proposed, but we saw a three-piece suite we liked and that clinched the idea.'

MOST PRACTICAL PROPOSAL

Even the dullest amongst us would be pressed to outdo the matter-of-factness mustered by Westminster School head master, Dr John Rae when putting the question to the woman of his dreams and future wife, Daphne.

Calling her from the head master's office at Harrow, where he had gone for a job interview, Rae cooed, 'I think the hierarchy might be afraid of homosexuality, as they prefer married men on the staff. There is an old condemned cottage in the Sanatorium grounds, which is empty. It's been suggested that we might get married at Christmas. How about it?'

Put like that, what else could a girl answer but 'Yes'?

LEAST ROMANTIC PROPOSAL

But Rae was down on bended knee to the sound of gypsy violin compared to the stunningly unromantic proposal put to the anonymous heroine of Daphne du Maurier's novel, *Rebecca*

'So Mrs Van Hopper has had enough of Monte Carlo', he said, 'and now she wants to go home. So do I. She to New York and I to Manderley. Which would you prefer? You can take your choice.'

'Do you mean you want a secretary or something?'

'No, I am asking you to marry me, you little fool.'

. . . 'So that's settled then, isn't it?', he said, going on with his toast and marmalade, 'instead of being companion to Mrs Van Hopper you become mine, and your duties will be almost exactly the same. The only difference is that I prefer Eno's, and you must never let me run out of my particular brand of toothpaste.'

LEAST IMMODEST CALL-GIRL

Dull folks, we've seen, 'do it' in bed. Some extremely dull prostitutes, however, don't do it at all.

One such was Alison Brown, who, fed up with being a typist, set up in business as 'The Virgin Call-Girl'.

Her working method, she told a magistrate, was to meet a client at an agreed venue and then, if she liked the look of him, ask for a deposit on future satisfaction.

'I found this worked rather well', she said, 'especially with foreigners.'

Then, she would simply not turn up.

'It was a bit mean really', she acknowledged, 'but as an unmarried mother I had my children to consider'.

LEAST EROTIC SEX FILM

Probably the least bawdy sex film ever made had the deceptively exciting title of *Furious Copulation*.

In the flesh – or, in practice, lack of it – however, it was so unarousing as on one occasion to arouse an entire audience of 600 Rio de Janeiro cinema-goers to rampage and smash the cinema showing it when the film's erotic highpoint proved to be the sight of a professor of the martial arts chasing a chicken.

MOST DISMAL SEXPERT

Victorian sexologist, Sir William Acton, was the dullest of a dismal breed. Even radical dulls today would not hold with all the views in his 1857 forerunner of *The Joy of Sex*, the best-selling, *Functions and Disorders of the Reproductive Organs*.

On the question of frequency Acton was clear. For an intellectual married man in London sexual congress was inadvisable more than once every ten days, or, if unavoidable, once a week.

For the man's wife, however, sexual congress was hardly advisable at all. 'She submits to her husband' wrote Acton, 'but only to please him; and, but for the desire of maternity, would far rather be relieved from his attentions.'

Acton's fantasy woman was a gigantically dull fish. As he remarked of one, 'She assured me that she felt no sexual passions whatsoever. Her passion for her husband was of a Platonic kind. I believe this lady is the perfect ideal of an English wife and mother.'

LEAST BAWDY MUSICAL REVUE

Following the success of the controversial, all-nude musical revue, *Oh Calcutta!*, a team of dull show people hit back in 1970 with a rather less controversial production called *Oh Gravesend!* in which the cast wore as many clothes as they could get on.

LEAST GOOEY PERSONAL AD

Dull men are romantic but not sentimental. (Let the lady get her own Milk Tray, they reckon.) Few less sentimental than the man responsible for a personal notice in the *Evesham Admag* in 1977.

'Young farmer with 100 acres would be pleased to hear from young lady with tractor. View to friendship, possibly matrimony. Please send photograph of tractor.'

LEAST SEDUCTIVE LOVE GIFT

Diamonds may be forever, and furs kind of nice but the way to socialist heroine, Rosa Luxemburg's heart was a really good economics textbook.

Or so she claimed in a refreshingly dull 1899 love letter to truelove, Leo Jogiches.

> I kiss you a thousand times for your dearest letter and
> present. . . . You simply cannot imagine how pleased I am with

your choice. Why, Rodbertus is simply my favourite economist and I can read him a hundred times for sheer intellectual pleasure . . .

LEAST GLITTERING WEDDING CEREMONY

Probably the least flashy wedding ever performed took place in Nashville, Tennessee in 1974.

The presiding official was Judge Charles Galbraith, to whom the intending couple explained they did not favour long, glitzy ceremonies.

'Do you want to get married?', the judge enquired. They did. 'You are.'

LEAST CONVENIENT TIME FOR LOVEMAKING

Love in the afternoon is all very fine but, for the dull, it is not always the uncomplicated affair it is cracked up to be.

One of its greatest drawbacks was encountered by a correspondent to the *Evening Standard*. 'Personally', she explained, 'I think night is the right time for married couples. But my husband often makes love to me in the afternoon, especially on Sundays, which puts me all behind with the washing-up.'

Un Chapter de Peter Freedman –
Dull Arts and Culture

'One of the biggest traps in showbusiness is to change
just because you've been doing something a long time.
What's wrong with being predictable?'

Val Doonican

On cultural matters, dull folks are broad-minded.

They are not the type, for instance, to refuse to see a film just
because it's in English, or colour.

Or to refuse to see a play or exhibition on the grounds that, they
never see ANYTHING *after* it's opened.

Dull folks, rather, are the easygoing, un-with-it types who
genuinely prefer painting by numbers to abstract expressionism and
Holiday on Ice to Pina Bausch's Dance Theatre of Wupperthal.

But for whom, finally, man does not live by art alone.

Film

The rule on films is, art students and Frenchmen go to 'Cinema',
Americans go to 'movies', and dull folks stay home and watch cousin
Noris's cine of 'Our Susan's' wedding to the trainee undermanager of
a gas showroom in Melton Mowbray.

That's what the art students and Frenchmen will tell you, anyway.

In fact, of course, dull folks have far broader tastes. They do,
however, like a film with a beginning, a middle and an end;
preferably in that order.

Which tends to rule out such efforts as *Une Femme et Un Subtitle*,
winner of the coveted Prix Tentious for its moving (albeit slowly)
story of a young French girl's love for an overweight subtitling
machine played by Gerard Depardieu.

As well, normally, as the latest season of experimental shorts by

final year students of the Albanian National Film School, following the Fetuccini retrospective mounted in *hommage* to one of the lesser-known *auteurs* of Italian neo-realism.

Dull folks, anyway, reckon that if a film was any good they would have made more than one of them. So they tend to like films with numbers in their names: *Breakdance II*, *Superman III*, *Rocky LCMXXVIII*, *Airport '77* (and yes, many have seen all previous 76).

The first question they ask, however, before going out to the cinema, is not, 'Who is the director?', but, 'Do they sell choc-ices?'. For in this age of mango sorbets and Shrimp Gumbo ice-cream, the Odeon and ABC are two of the few places a person can still get a proper vanilla fruit parfait or real Kia-ora orange.

The question they sometimes *get* asked is, why bother going at all, what with the cost and the hassle? Art students and Frenchmen answer back something about the magic of the big screen, the thrill of 12-inch subtitles. Dull folks know that of all the magic thrills of the movies, none can really compare with the barely suspended disbelief – if not sheer screaming exhilaration – of actually getting through on the phone to the cinema box office.

Dull folks have not seen *The Rocky Horror Picture Show* 238 times and know every line by heart. They have not seen it once.

Other films they do not know by heart are *The Draughtsman's Contract, Swann in Love* (or anything with Jeremy Irons), *The Man Who Fell to Earth* (ditto David Bowie), or any film directed by someone with too many names: Jean-Luc Godard, Pierre Paolo Pasolini or Rainer Werner Fassbinder.

The films *they* know by heart are *The Sound of Music* (or anything with Julie Andrews), *Ordinary People* and the industrial training film on fire and safety regulations in government buildings they see every year at work.

MOST HONEST ADMISSION

'My heart tells me the negative was smuggled out of some distant, oppressed country under the noses of a vicious totalitarian regime, but the numbness in my backside tells me I would be better off at home watching Sportsnight.'

Director, Alan Parker (or, at least, a cartoon of his).

Music

Dull folks like music with a tune. They like a tune they can hum.

The eight records *they* would take on a desert island therefore are the following dull hits:

The Sun Has Got Its Hat On

All Things Bright and Beautiful (music to their ears)

Spread a Little Happiness

And Sheep May Safely Graze (one they just never tire of)

These Are a Few of My Favourite Things

Have Yourself a Merry Little Christmas, by Sid Laurence and his Orchestra

Oh, No John, No John, No John, No

The K-tel compilation of twelve classic theme-tunes for the first time on one album, (with the themes to The Archers, the BBC World Service News, Rugby Special and Stars on Sunday particular favourites).

NOTE: Dull folks were never amongst those who campaigned for a

special tax on Cliff Richard records or the abolition of Tony Blackburn. (*They* always felt it a pity when Tony Blackburn interrupted the banter to play a record.) Or amongst those who have now rediscovered them. As it is, they like them both, though they suspect for the wrong reasons.

Theatre

Dull theatregoers know that man does not live by Brecht alone. Or even by Stoppard or Pinter. Man lives also by Alan Ayckbourn, Agatha Christie and Andrew Lloyd-Webber.

Dull folks like a play with a plot. They like a play with a story. They like a play with a set, dialogue and characters.

They therefore tend not to like those plays by Samuel Beckett in which there is no plot, story, set, dialogue or characters, and nothing happens – for three hours. These, they reckon, are the true Theatre of Cruelty.

Dull folks accept the show must go on. But must it, they ask, go on and on?

They have little wish therefore to see five hour plays by nineteenth-century Scandinavians with angst in their pants. Or the 'uncut version' of anything. They may be willing to suffer for their art, but only for so long.

Dull folks haven't 'seen it on Broadway'. Or 'with Olivier at Stratford in '54'. Nor do they spend every interval circulating in the crush bar, muttering to the Japanese tourists, 'Of course, not as good as the book', even when they haven't read the book or there never *was* a book.

Literature

When Dame Edith Evans heard that smart-set novelist Nancy Mitford had been lent a villa to finish a book her natural reaction was, 'Oh really? What exactly is she reading?'

Dull folks know what she meant.

It would be wrong to say dull folks live by the rule, 'If you can't buy it in a station bookstall it's not worth reading'. Let's just say, it may not be insignificant that you won't find *The Unbearable Lightness of Being* by Milan Kundera in that many station bookstalls.

Beyond that, dull folks like their poetry to rhyme and their novels to have a story.

Until the Book Marketing Council, however, produces its list of the Twenty Dullest Young British Authors their reading is largely restricted to the following library of dull classics:

- *Glad to be Grey* (the dull bible)
- *Diary of a Nobody* (*the* dull classic)
- *The Observer Book of Birds*
- *Exchange & Mart*
- *The Times* Special Supplements on the Nigerian banking system
- *The Daily Telegraph* Church News column
- Colour supplement series on 'A Day in a Room I Wish I'd Lived in at 18', or variation thereof.
- The Reader's Digest condensed version of almost anything.
- Most things by James Herriot, Percy Thrower and Agatha Christie (but few things by Milan Kundera, Salman Rushdie, Jack Kerouac, Albert Camus, Søren Kierkegaard, Gabriel Garcia Marquez, Faber and Faber or Janet Street Porter).

Television

While in other areas of the arts dull folks are not that up-to-date, when it comes to television, they live for the moment.

Thus, they watch *Dallas* and *Dynasty* first time round, instead of waiting for them to resurface in some National Film Theatre retrospective in twenty years time.

They also watched *The Twilight Zone, The Man from Uncle, The Munsters, The Adams Family* and *The Mary Tyler Moore Show* when they were all first on – like, for real, and at the time, when all the art students and croissant-dunkers who now rave about them on Channel Four and late-night BBC2 rated anyone who had even heard of TV as a pea-brained squarehead.

NOTE: As far as dull folks are concerned, *Dallas* is about Who shot JR? and *Coronation Street* about whether Deirdre will make up her latest tiff with Ken – *not* about 'the notion of a text being a fixed unit of meaning which is organised by an underlying structural system of binary oppositions', as a recent British Film Institute Media Studies course tried to claim.

93

The great and the dull – dull cultural heroes

– Ex-President Gerald Ford for hearing the name Mick Jagger, and reportedly asking, 'Isn't he that motorcycle rider?'
– Journalist Miles Kington for announcing in 1967 that he could not stand either Bob Dylan or the Rolling Stones and losing thirty friends in an evening.
– Neasden's Queen of Soul Mari Wilson for declaring her ambitions to be 'a week at the Palladium' (since achieved) and 'a complete set of Pyrex and Tupperware'.
– Birmingham's Queen of Rock Joan Armatrading for being not just a shy, teetotalling former computer programmer but, by her own admission, 'quite straight-laced'.
– Hollywood's Master of Suspense Alfred Hitchcock for admitting of life in tinsel town, 'We lead a very suburban life here. We're in bed by nine o'clock every night.'
– Poet George Herbert for pointing out in one of the great dull proverbs that, 'Music helps not the toothache'.
– Puritan Oliver Cromwell for banning the theatre on grounds of general sinfulness.
– General Ulysees S. Grant for being asked whether he had enjoyed a concert and answering, 'How could I? I know only two tunes. One of them is "Yankee Doodle" and the other isn't.'
– Novelist Emily Brontë for being a famously dull fish, of whom Edith Sitwell on one occasion recalled, 'The daughters of a Dr Wheelwright would have liked to go about with Charlotte, if only dull Emily could have been left behind.'
– Actress Sheila Gish for reflecting, 'I wish I did something extraordinary, like keep a crocodile in the bath', but confessing, 'One is very ordinary.'

Radio

On the radio the dull listen to:

David Jacobs's *Melodies For You* on Radio 2

Gardeners' Question Time and *Time for Verse* on Radio 4

The late-night phone-in on Radio Anything

But not Robert Robinson and his cronies sitting around trying to revive the art of conversation on *Stop the Week*.

Unsung heroes of dullness

LEAST GUILTY TELEVISION JUNKIES

'My philosophy', says Neasden's Queen of Soul Mari Wilson, 'is you can only watch one TV at a time.'

The Couch Potatoes are a Californian sect of committed television watchers who don't agree. *Their* philosophy is, 'There is no such thing as too much TV' – or too many TV sets. Couch Potato heaven is watching a dozen sets, tuned to as many channels, in one orgiastic session of 'simul-viewing'.

But their essential message is merely that watching TV is nothing to be ashamed of. TV viewers, in common with their kindred spirit, the dull, have been maligned, ridiculed and persecuted for too long.

Says Jack Mingo, author of the sect's manual and – after the TV Times – most sacred text, *Official Couch Potato Handbook*, 'Even in the 1960s when women, gays and other stigmatised groups came out of the closet, TV viewing was still a dirty little secret for millions.'

It's time now, he says, to stop feeling guilty. Time to stop lying about how much TV we watch. (Mingo himself admits to, or rather, boasts of, eighteen hours a day.) Time to View with Dignity. Time for Couch Potatoes everywhere to lie down and be counted.

LEAST SCINTILLATING POET

Alfred Lord Tennyson was not the kind of poet wracked by turbulent, obsessive moods. Nor the sort a hostess could rely on to light up any salon. Truth to tell, he was rather on the dull side.

As author F. Anstey was fond of illustrating with the story of a young admirer of the poet's who, staying on one occasion with the Tennysons, was one afternoon to her considerable excitement invited to step out in the garden with the great man.

The two strolled together for some time in silence. He did not speak, she assumed, on account of some important meditation and she said nothing for fear of missing some poetic gem. They had come full circle when Tennyson suddenly and without preliminaries observed, 'Coals are very dear.'

She could think of no apt reply and so instead chose to use their second circuit of the garden to dwell on the remark. She had just about digested it, and they just about come round a second time, when Tennyson again burst forth. 'I get all my meat from London,' he said.

This took his companion equally aback. She had regained her composure, however, by the time the poet stopped suddenly once more beside a crop of ailing carnations. She, relates Anstey, waited hopefully for a remark she would always treasure. Pronounced Tennyson, 'It's those cursed rabbits', his final offering of the day.

LEAST AVANT-GARDE POET

Derrière-garde poet Nigel Frith is a man unimpressed by twentieth-century literature. James Joyce he describes as, 'bloody awful . . . labouring to be trivial.' As for Ezra Pound, 'He was a crackpot. Yeats is second rate but the rest are fourth-rate.'

Things for Frith, in fact, have been going down hill since Homer, as he told reporters during a second unsuccessful campaign to become Oxford Professor of Poetry, in 1978.

Under one local press headline to the effect that, 'Art's a Fart', and alongside a portrait of the poet eating a copy of Joyce's *A Portrait of the Artist as a Young Man*, the no-nonsense Frith explained, 'I can't bear modern poetry. It makes me sick. Let's get the intellectuals.'

He was little keener on modern art. 'Modern art is rubbish', he argued. 'The people who just draw a green line around a canvas are barking mad.'

In the event, Frith's bid to become Oxford's top poet may have been hampered by the decision to base his campaign on his prose writing. 'I do write poetry', he pointed out. He simply didn't consider it as significant a part of his output.

LEAST EXOTIC TRAVELOGUE

As far as dull folks are concerned there is more to cinema than glamour and excitement – long ticket queues for example, and, above all, the travelogues from the Greek National Tourist Board portraying simple mountain villages, unchanged and unchanging (i.e. dull) for thousands of years, where simple mountain villagers eke out a meagre living from the thankless soil before returning nights to their simple white-washed dwellings gaily dotted with rusting television aerials.

One of the great dull travelogues of recent years was made by a young director by the name of Michael Winner. It was a small-budget affair with the promisingly unexotic title of *This is Belgium*. So small budget, as it proved, that for much of the action the part of Belgium was taken by East Grinstead.

LEAST ENGROSSING EXPERIMENTAL BOOK

Even dull authors will sometimes want to try something different and new. In the case of ninety-one year-old chiropractor and author, Mrs Marva Drew it was a chance remark of a patient's that inspired her magnum and innovative opus, finished in 1974.

'He said that nobody could count up to a million', she explained to *The San Francisco Chronicle*. 'He was wrong'.

As Mrs Drew proved in what she described as an 'experimental' book, composed by her typing out every number from one to a million.

'It took me five years and over 60 reams of paper', said the Iowan author.

LEAST PRICELESS MUSEUM EXHIBIT

One of the world's least valuable objets d'art is a jelly-mould.

When the donation of the mould for display in Bournemouth's Russell-Cotes Museum was discussed by the town's Art Galleries and Museums Sub-Committee in 1980, the anti-mould lobby was led by a Mrs Eunice Wentworth.

The mould, she said, had been bought by its girl-guide donor from a local jumble sale for one pound. Even at that price, however, Mrs Wentworth felt it had not been a bargain. 'The people who threw it out did not want it', she told the meeting and *Bournemouth Evening Echo*. 'We do not want it. Nobody wants it. It is not wanted, period.'

Rallying in the mould's defence, Councillor Harvey Topham spoke eloquently of the prodigality of our throw-away society. 'Too many people today are only too happy to throw everything out', he said. 'This sort of rare item is of great educational interest and will be admired by thousands of' – presumably dull – 'teenagers.'

LEAST FUSSY CINEMA-GOER

Ailing British cinemas could do with customers of the loyalty of Florida security guard Paul Morgan.

When the press caught up with Morgan in 1974, he had been attending his local picture house every afternoon, come comedy or thriller, come subtitle or no, for twenty-five years.

He first stopped by, he told reporters, one afternoon in 1949 because he was bored. By now, however, it had become what he described as 'a habit'.

He refused to be drawn on any single film that had stuck in his mind after an estimated 55,000 hours viewing. His memory was not what it had been, he said. 'And in any case, I spend a lot of the time asleep.'

After saying that he planned to carry on going until he retired in 1977, Morgan confessed, 'I do not like films very much. They certainly stir up violence.'

LEAST ROUSING POEM ON THE DULLNESS OF LIFE

Far from being one long Martini commercial, dull folks know that life is more like one long accountancy exam.

As was well put by nineteenth-century poet, Ben King in his anthem to the dullness of life, 'The Pessimist',

Nothing to do but work,
Nothing to eat but food,
Nothing to wear but clothes
To keep one from going nude.

Nothing to breathe but air
Quick as a flash 'tis gone;
Nowhere to fall but off,
Nowhere to stand but on.

Nothing to comb but hair,
Nowhere to sleep but in bed,
Nothing to weep but tears,
Nothing to bury but dead.

Nothing to sing but songs,
Ah, well, alas! alack!
Nowhere to go but out,
Nowhere to come but back.

LEAST SWINGING FILM STAR

While hipper movie stars hang out at Studio 54 or loose in their backseat Jacuzzis, cowboy star, Gene Autrey remains a dull hero for laying down what is still one of the great dull behaviour codes.

The ten commandments themselves are a recipe for loose living beside the 'Gene Autrey 10-point Cowboy Code':

1 A cowboy never takes unfair advantage – even of an enemy
2 A cowboy never betrays a trust
3 A cowboy always tells the truth
4 A cowboy is kind to small children, to old folks and to animals
5 A cowboy is free from racial and religious prejudice
6 A cowboy is helpful and, when anyone's in trouble he lends a hand
7 A cowboy is a good worker
8 A cowboy is clean about his person and in thought, word and deed
9 A cowboy respects womanhood, his parents and the laws of his country
10 A cowboy is a patriot

MOST INOFFENSIVE REVIEW

One of the most damningly inoffensive reviews in theatrical history was the one-line newspaper verdict on a production of *Fresh Fields* by Ivor Novello at the Criterion Theatre in 1933.

'The frocks', it read, 'were charming.'

LEAST GLAMOROUS FILM FESTIVAL

The Hull Film Festival never set out to be the Cannes of the North. And yet, right from that first afternoon in spring, 1985 when Mrs Worsley, assistant manageress of the Hull ABC, fetched out the old bunting and personally took charge of washing and ironing it before decking the cinema, the world film community knew it had witnessed the branding of a new date on its key festival calendar.

That first ever, if as yet not terribly prestigious, Hull Film Festival, opened with an official gala lunch attended by a galaxy of international stars including . . . well, Michael Palin came along with a pig from his film, *A Private Function*, courtesy of Northern Pig Developments.

But the true Humberside flavour of the festival perhaps best shone through when Palin and fellow star, Terry Gilliam, forewent such traditional film feste rituals as cocktails on the terrace of Cannes' Carlton Terrace Hotel or spritzers on the Lido seafront in favour of a glass of homemade grapefruit wine in the projection room of the seventy-four-year-old Beverly Picture Playhouse, before seeing snaps of the recent staff outing to Hornsea.

'Do you have Dolby stereo?', Gilliam asked manager, Peter Robinson. 'We've only just got talkies', answered Robinson, whose seats date back to 1935.

The festival went on to see not only the town's first ever unrestricted screening of Monty Python's *Life of Brian*, still officially banned in Hull, but also the world premiere of a short film about Hull City Tigers football team.

'It has reawakened people's interest in the cinema', said Hull Film Theatre manager, Alf Wilson, who had met one old man making his first ever visit to the Film Theatre. 'He said to me, "I've had a cup of tea this afternoon and I've seen a nice film. I've come this evening, had a choc-ice and seen another good film and it's not even my birthday." '

So that, by the time the news came through in mid-feste of the *Hull Daily Mail's* offer to sponsor a sequel in 1986, the question no longer seemed to be whether Hull could yet become the Cannes of the North, but whether Cannes could ever hope to become the Hull of France.

LEAST INSPIRED MULTI-MEDIA ARTISTE

It falls to few dull artistes to achieve in their lifetime not only their country's first ever million-selling single but also a title role in that country's most unbewitchingly titled film.

Such was the versatility, and such the dullness of Chinese leader, Chairman Mao, however, that only the most revisionist of counter-revolutionaries were surprised to see him follow his hit single, *Sing Along With Mao* (featuring crooned extracts from his bestseller, *The Little Red Book*) with a star part in China's answer to *Breakdance III – Chairman Mao Reviews the Mighty Contingent of the Cultural Revolution for the 5th and 6th Times*.

LEAST ENTICING FILM TITLES

The only film titles ever known to set quite as few hearts-a-flutter or spines-a-tingle were:

– *The Longest and Most Meaningless Movie in the World,* a British counter-culture film made in 1970, which in its full forty-eight hour version was indeed the longest and most meaningless movie in the world. And, from China again,
– *I Was Women's Basketball Champion from Collective Number Nine.*

And finally from Britain again, no less than that country's first ever film – made in 1888 and entitled, – *Traffic Crossing Leeds Bridge.*

LEAST EXCITING COMPOSER AND CONCERT

French composer Erik Satie not only dressed in a drab and repetitive way – his wardrobe consisted of thirteen identical dark grey suits – but seemed to go out of his way to write unexciting music.

Of all his work, the most ostentatiously uninteresting was his composition, 'Vexations'. This comprised one sheet of tuneless music to be repeated 840 times.

When musicians Adrian Fish and Dawn Pye gave a rare performance of the piece in a recent concert in Presteigne, Wales the rendition lasted seventeen hours, not including a brief encore.

MOST UNDERWHELMED THEATRE-GOER

The story is told in theatrical circles of the dull theatre-goer attending an 1892 performance of Sarah Bernhardt's *Cleopatra.*

The great actress was in savage form that night. After a performance of unbridled passion, Bernhardt climaxed the evening by smashing the royal palace and collapsing histrionically in the ruins – managing, in quick succession, to bring down the set, the curtain and the house.

Amid the scenes of audience rapture, the voice of one under-wrought female patron was heard to reflect with quiet gratification.

'How different, how very different from the home life of our own dear Queen.'

LEAST GLAMOROUS VIEWING METHOD

Dull folks know that there is room for only so many of us in the royal box at the opera or seats next to the stage at a gig.

The rest of us must find our own ways and places to enjoy the arts we enjoy. Some, like Eastbourne woman and *Jackanory* fan, Mrs Brenda Winkle find humbler ways than others.

'I have been watching Jackanory through Thompson's window for the last three months', she told a magistrate after being charged with using a pair of scissors as an offensive weapon in the attempt to clear her view of the screen. 'I didn't want to miss a moment of it.'

Thompson's, she pointed out, put the set out as a customer service. She had been a customer for three decades.

She therefore felt no compunction in using her scissors to stab fellow viewer, Miss Joan Naylor in the bottom. Miss Naylor had not only been at the front of the crowd, she said, but wouldn't stop bobbing about blocking the screen.

'In any case', concluded Mrs Winkle in her own defence, 'she's 20 and I am 73, so I am allowed to teach her a lesson.'

LEAST HIP FILM CENSORS

This accolade falls to the British Board of Censors for, in its 1930's heyday, banning such beastly unscreenables as 'immodesty', 'British officers shown in an unflattering light' and (unspecified) 'vulgar noises'.

And for, in a moment of sweet revenge for hours of painful viewing refusing a certificate to the French film, *The Seashell and the Clergyman* on the grounds that, 'This film is apparently meaningless. (But) If there is any meaning it is doubtless objectionable.'

THE WORLD'S DULLEST BOOKSHOP

Nicholas Willmott's bookshop in St Nicholas Street, Ipswich is both a shrine to the achievements of dull publishers and authors and a refuge for books too uninteresting to be wanted by the outside world.

A History of Harlow, How to Run a Bassoon Factory and *The Lighter Side of Local Government* were never works destined to set the pulse racing or publishing world alight. But Wilmott has given them all a roof over the years and been proud to do it.

Some of the books he takes in, such as *Out and About With Undertakers*, are quickly found new homes. That was sold to the mother of an apprentice undertaker. For others, like *An Irishman's Difficulties With the Irish Language* demand exceeds supply.

But others still are likely to see out their days on Wilmott's shelves. Even a major promotion and window display failed to stir interest in *The Human Side of Insurance*. Response to the shop's signed copy of *The Story of Luton* has been equally disappointing.

Margarine is a recurring theme of his acquisitions, of which the most recent is a volume on *The Social History of Margarine*. But of which the proudest was a pamphlet he found a few years ago listing *Some Interesting Facts About Margarine*. Not only because it seemed almost to suggest that certain other facts about margarine might be less than interesting, but also because it bagged him second prize in an odd title competition (won by a technical work on organ construction called *The Big Problem of Small Organs*).

Other specialties include Czech editions of P.G. Wodehouse and less useful colonial phrase books, of which *Forbes' Hindustani Manual* and *An Easy Introduction to Colloquial Bengali* are his prides. The latter lists such key phrases as, 'A man who has a cow speaks straight' and, 'He doesn't know how to dance so it is the fault of the courtyard.'

But the one book Willmott says he'll never part with is *The Crows of Shakespeare*. This is a volume of crow illustrations by a Mrs Hugh Blackmore – one for each time her favourite bird is mentioned in the complete works. The book's real beauty, though, he says, is that Mrs Blackmore had almost no drawing ability; as she confessed in an earlier work, *A Few Words about Drawing for Beginners after a Long Experience of its Difficulties*.

Willmott also sidelines in unenticing book blurbs. His favourite is the come-on for detective writer, Sydney Horler's thriller, *The Charlatan*. It begins, 'Mr Horler has chosen as his theme the conflict between the recognised medical profession and the practitioners of osteopathy . . .'. Notes the bookseller, 'The copy we've got has never been read'.

Willmott has sworn not to rest until he finds copies of such grails as *Fish Who Answer the Telephone* and *The True Inwardness of the Oyster*. Or of a work he mentions in hushed tones as reportedly having surfaced in a recent exhibition in York: *The Catalogue of Valves in the Royal Liver Building, Liverpool*.

LEAST ARRESTING BOOK TITLES

It is said in America that the list of twelve books with which to launch a publishing firm sure to fail would be headed by, *Canada, Our Good Neighbour to the North*. Here the equivalent title might be, *The Years of Restraint: Geoffrey Howe's Collected Budget Speeches, 1979–83*.

But among volumes that have actually seen the light of print, is there or could there be a less entrancingly titled volume than, *A Million Random Digits with 100,000 Normal Deviates by The Rand*

Corporation, Beginning with 3174388901 and Ending with 216847593? (Some of the middle passages, one is advised, can be skipped.)

The closest this publisher could come would be its definitive study of *Medieval Mousetraps and Other Spring Mechanisms.* And even writer, Robert Benchley, who spent a lifetime collecting books with uninteresting titles came up with nothing less exciting than, *Talks on Manure, Keeping a Single Cow* and *The Culture and Diseases of the Sweet Potato.*

If a challenger is to be found to *A Million Random Digits with 100,000 Normal Deviates by the Rand Corporation Beginning with 3174388901 and Ending with 216847593* then it is likely to emerge from the titles spotted by the panel reporting back each year to *The Bookseller* magazine on odd and unenthralling titles at the Frankfurt Book Fair.

Among the only marginally unriveting titles of recent Frankfurts have been:

– *How to Thoroughly Criticise the Gang of Four and Bring About a New Upsurge in the Movement to Build Tachai-Type Counties Throughout the Country* (China)
– *The Interpretation of Geological Times from the Evidence of Fossilized Elephant Droppings in Eastern Europe* (Poland, but now published in four languages)
– *Proceedings of the Second International Workshop on Nude Mice* (Japan)
– *Nasal Maintenance: Nursing Your Nose through Troubled Times* (US)
– *The Theory of Lengthwise Rolling* (USSR)
– *A Colour Atlas of Posterior Chamber Implants* (UK)
– *Goodbye to the Flush Toilet: Water-Saving Alternatives to Cesspools, Septic Tank and Sewers* (UK)
– *Marmalade: Its Antecedents, Its History and Its Role in the World Today* (UK)

But the list of those books which once put down just could not be picked up again was headed by:

– *Big and Very Big Hole Drilling* (UK)
– *Picture Your Dog in Needlework* (UK)
– *Living With Antiques in New Zealand* (NZ)
– *100 Years of British Rail Catering* (UK) and
– *Also and Too: A Corpus-Based Study of Their Frequency and Use in Modern English* (Sweden)

Dull Moments in History, as Captured in . . .

The dullest ever headlines

'NOVA SCOTIA NOT TO GO ENTIRELY METRIC'
blazed the headline in *The Canadian Government Review* late
in 1983.

I suppose that as long as we live none of us will ever
remember where we were or what we were doing when we
first heard the news that one of Canada's smallest provinces
had decided partially to postpone its proposed metrication
programme.

Yet this is the stuff that *real* history is made of – the
unremarkable moments of ordinary folks and minor local
governments going about their not particularly special or
exciting lives.

This is the stuff the history books *should* be filled with.
Because, for every great battle and violent revolution, every
dramatic turning point that changed history and each Ten
Days that Shook the World, the fact is, there were tens of
thousands of days and billions of moments that shook no one
and changed nowt.

These are the moments which make up the yet unwritten
History of the Dull – the moments neglected by 'dullist'
history books but captured at least in some cases and recent
years by contemporary headlines . . .

THE WEATHER IS COMPLETELY NORMAL
The least earth-shattering headline imaginable was always
supposed to be the one which won journalist, Claude
Cockburn a famous boring headline competition amongst
staff of *The Times*: SMALL EARTHQUAKE IN CHILE – NOT MANY
DEAD.

But apart from the fact of the recent *large* earthquake in
Chile which left *many* dead and hence Cockburn's headline
no longer so boring, even to start with it was never the match
of such as:
– (The well-known but perhaps apocryphal because untrace-
able) DEAD MAN FOUND IN GRAVEYARD.
– APATHY STRIKES TORBAY (*Torbay News*, 1981)

NEWSPAPER SELLER'S WIFE RUNS OFF WITH MAN FROM COUNCIL WHO CAME TO UNBLOCK THE DRAINS

But the best collection of recent unmemorable headlines were those entered for a 1982 competition run by *The Observer*'s 'Pendennis' column.

Among the only moderately unexciting entries were:

- IMMATERIAL DECEPTION DOES NOT VITIATE LEAVE TO ENTER
(*The Times* – Winner of the 'Unintelligible As Well as
Unexciting' Category)
- CYCLIST HAD TO BRAKE (*Kentish Gazette*)
- FISH AND CHIPS ENJOYED AT EDGBASTON WOMEN ZIONISTS
BAZAAR (*Birmingham Jewish Chronicle*)
- LITTLE CHANGE IN 21 YEARS (*Express and Star*)
- CHURCH CLOCK DID NOT STOP 40 YEARS AGO (*The Messenger*,
Stockport)
- FEW INDIAN FILMS MAKE IT TO NEW ZEALAND (*Statesman*,
India)
- OSWESTRY MAYOR PLANTS A TREE (*Shropshire Star*)
- FORMER DEPUTY MAYOR OF RUGBY TWIN TOWN DIES (*Rugby
Advertiser*)

But these were cause for hats to be thrown in the air and
bells to peel in celebration compared to the two beaten
finalists which, in reverse order, were:
- WORLD HAS WARMED BY 0.4F SINCE 1965 (*The Times*, 2
September, 1981)
- LIECHSTENSTEIN'S EXPORTS SHOW FALL OF 0.6% (*The Financial
Times*, 21 May, 1982)

It was, however, journalists on the Austrian paper, the
Kurier who one uneventful November evening in 1977, held
the front page for the winning headline . . .

THE WEATHER IS COMPLETELY NORMAL

Dull Folks Say Relax –
Dull Sports and Hobbies

'If only Hitler and Mussolini could have a good game of bowls once a week at Geneva I feel that Europe would not be as troubled as it is.'

War-time MP, Captain R.G. Bristow

Dull folks do not believe 'you only live once'. (Or therefore say things like, 'If I only have one life let me live it as a chiropodist.') Which is not to say they believe in reincarnation. Merely that they don't believe you should 'try everything once'. Or that 'everything's an experience'. Some things are definitely not an experience. Among those things which are not experiences are:

* Bungy-jumping off the Golden Gate Bridge
* Skate-boarding before the bulls of Pamplona
* Bobsleighing down the Cresta Run on a lavatory seat
* Walking tightrope between the twin towers of the New York World Trade Centre
* Skiing down Everest naked with a carnation between your teeth.

Dull folks, in short, do not go in for show-off hobbies and breakneck sports in the quest for expensive thrills.

Even given the cash, death and serious injury simply do not figure among the ways they like to relax.

How then do dull folks relax?

Dull folks knit. They Do-It-Themselves. They spot trains and rub brasses. They trim the herbaceous border.

They go bell-ringing, morris dancing and pottering on their allotment but not abseiling, parasailing, hang-gliding, scuba-diving,

ski-jumping or hot-dogging. When dull folks relax they like to be able to relax.

They go ponytrekking but not ice-trekking and golfing but not Rolfing.

Travel writers go big-game hunting and deep-sea fishing. Dull folks prefer bird-watching and gravel-pit angling.

They play bowls, cricket, croquet and billiards. And draughts, bridge, cribbage and progressive whist. They make jam and build matchstick boats.

Dull folks play Scrabble rather than backgammon and Monopoly but not Trivial Pursuit.

In pubs they play traditional games but not so traditional that they went extinct in nineteenth-century Staffordshire, when no one much enjoyed them either. Down the local they play darts or Andy Williams on the jukebox.

Dull folks go swimming – in the municipal baths, not solo across the Atlantic.

They play pin-ball – but don't write rock musicals about it.

DULL EXERCISE

As far as exercise classes go dull folks don't see why they should fork out good money to do the very thing they spent the best years of their lives forging sicknotes to avoid.

They especially avoid such designer classes as 'Slimnastics', 'Dancercise', 'Jazzercise' and doing what Jane Fonda terms 'Little Bouncers for the Buttocks'.

'Aerobics is dead', say the papers. Dull folks say, 'What's Aerobics?'

If they do exercises at all, they will be the Canadian Airforce Exercises in the shower each morning before breakfast, as they have done them ever since they were in the Canadian Airforce.

My other car's also a Volvo – dulls hit the road

Dull folks ask of a car only that it should:

* Get them where they need to go
* Fit more than a half pound bag of kiwi fruit in the back seat
* Do 0–60 without needing a fuel stop
* Not leave them a stain on the tarmac on collision with a Sinclair C5 electrically assisted tricycle.

Whether or not a car is capable of doing the double ton round the chicane at Silverstone or Gucci to Fiorucci in 4.8 seconds are not considerations.

Which tends to rule out the flash, foreign cars with too little leg room and cricket score price tags driven by overweight rock stars and commercials directors – the kind capable of speeds exceeding Mach II on a pre-dawn autobahn, but incapable of not boiling over while waiting their turn at an experimental mini-roundabout.

The only automobile, in fact, that meets all their requirements is the classic Volvo Estate with front and rear crumple zones – the dull dream machine; as well as the only foreign car they'd dream of driving.

NOTE: As on the beach, so on the road, dulls don't go topless. Porsche-drivers with wind-blown hair and leathery faces have convertibles. Dull folks have sunroofs.

Unsung heroes of dullness

LEAST EXHILARATING SPORT

Faster than a dawdle but slower than a stroll, a saunter might best be described as a leisurely and aimless mosey.

As a sport sauntering overlaps with ambling, rambling, meandering and plain walking but it is also now a distinct and recognized discipline overseen by the American-based World Saunter Society.

Highlight of the sauntering year is the Society's big annual August saunter along the porch – said to be the world's longest – of the Grand Hotel, Mackinac Island. The event, it must be stressed, is not

The great and the dull – dull sports and hobby heroes

– Film star Victor Mature for being asked, 'What do you do in your spare time?, and answering, 'I sit around a lot.' And,

– Rock star Eric Clapton for agreeing, 'Given the choice between accomplishing something and just lying around, I'd rather lie around. No contest.'

– Brown bomber Joe Louis for listing his favourite hobby as 'sleeping'.

– Racing driver Alain de Cadenet, for confessing, 'I actually get more excited collecting stamps than I do racing cars'.

– The late Eric Morecambe, for being an avid birdwatcher, and commenting, 'I find it very relaxing and it doesn't harm anyone. I think it's great.' And,

– Jazz musician Humphrey Lyttelton for agreeing, 'I can spend hours watching sparrows'.

– Fashion designer Hardy Amies for his passion for needlepoint.

– The late Lord Wolfenden for listing his recreations in *Who's Who* as 'Walking About' (1971), 'Getting used to retirement' (1975), 'Weeding' (1978), 'Waiting to cross the A25 on foot' (1980) and 'Trying to come to terms with arthritis, bifocals and dentures' (1983).

– The Queen for her love of stamp collecting and jigsaw puzzles.

– The royal family for being fiends for a game of Scrabble.

a race. Speed and competition are anathema to saunterers.

Sauntering has most of the benefits of jogging without the risks – the gain without the pain and fun and relaxation without the need for expensive or indeed any special gear. Walking sticks, umbrellas and cardigans are all used but the basic philosophy is come as you are and saunter as and where you feel comfortable.

It was, say saunterers, the ancient Greeks who pioneered the sport on their long pedagogical saunters. Given the hours he put in holding forth to students on his famous group mosies, experts believe Aristotle could have sauntered for Greece.

But it is only this century that sauntering has caught on at a mass level, at first on the decks of cruise liners and city pavements among after-dinner practioners; and now under the auspices of the World Saunter Society. Maurice Chevalier and Oliver Hardy are two modern greats.

It is a sport any one can enjoy, whatever age or condition. For the novice as for the experienced saunterer, the Society's advice is, 'Start slowly, saunter slowly, stop slowly, live longer.'

LEAST OVER-THE-MOON GAMBLER

'I had to work on my allotment and feed the chickens', explained assistant seed exporter, Frank Bradley after failing to pick up £91,000 race winnings from his bookmaker in 1978. 'I just couldn't fit it in.'

MOST POINTLESS AND UNEXCITING PASTIME

Sitting around (see Victor Mature), lying around (see Eric Clapton) and, most strenuous, standing or 'hanging' around are three of the great dull pastimes.

In each activity, however, the choice of venue is crucial. Hanging around in a Covent Garden winebar being witty and amusing, for instance, just isn't the same as hanging around on a shabby street corner doing nothing in particular – as was the hobby of New Yorker and dull hero, Joseph Carroll.

Carroll used to scurry home from the office each day, change into a suitably drab dark suit and hat, and shuffle off to stand around on one or other street corner. His favourite was the corner of Fourth Street and Jane, on which he stood around man and boy, rain and shine for thirty-three years without once saying why.

MOST DEATHLY DULL BLOOD SPORT

Dull folks do not normally favour violent or bloody sports. That even death can be dull, however, was demonstrated by the less than intrepid hunters of the Florida Wildlife Association.

'We cater to the armchair hunter', was how Association chairman, George McHugh described the group in 1978.

In essence, this involved buying up ageing lions and tigers and long-in-the-tooth leopards and cougars from zoos around the country wanting shot of them. Then placing them in cages and shooting them.

The shooting was done from chairs positioned near to the cage for maximum accuracy and minimum effort. Originally, the Association used to let their game out of their cages before killing them. But this proved unpopular with both parties. Explained McHugh, 'The animals didn't want to run about and the hunters didn't want to chase them'.

LEAST EXCITING BOXING MATCH

Runner-up for this honour was the memorably uneventful bare-knuckle bout staged last century in Canada between English champ, Jim Mace and US challenger, Joe Coburn. When the contest was finally abandoned after one hour and seventeen minutes there was little to choose between the two sluggers, neither having landed a single punch.

But for more concentrated lack of excitement this was no match for the 1977 Golden Gloves contest between American bantam-weights, Harvey Garley and Dennis Outlette. From the opening bell, Garley came out dancing and bobbing. Which he continued to do for a full forty-seven seconds before unleashing his first, and, as it proved, last punch of the night, missing his opponent but bringing himself crashing to the canvas, out for the count.

LEAST THRILLING BULLFIGHT

The least exhilarating bullfight in Spanish history was fought, or at least, held, at Madrid's Vista Alegre bullring in 1973.

Dull heroes of the day were peace-loving matador, Diego Bardon and a no less placid bull. As his opening and, as it proved, most provocative gesture of the afternoon, Bardon tossed a bunch of flowers almost directly at his opponent. Then, by way of apology for this unwarranted aggression, he performed a solo dance of conspicuous sensitivity and grace.

While a more passionate toro might have been disconcerted by this display, on this occasion Bardon had met his equal. The bull gave as good as it got, not only openly declining Bardon's bouquet and grazing instead on some flowers growing wild in the ring but then, in a gesture of unambiguous defiance, loping off to the far edge of the arena.

After further thrust and counter thrust in a similar vein, the crowd's amusement curdled into anger. Finally, our heros were ushered from the ring, moments before a probable lynching.

The bull was not formally censured but Bardon was charged and imprisoned under the Spanish law which requires a matador at least try to kill the bull in a bullfight.

In his day, Bardon had killed 100 bulls. That, however, was before enlisting in a new movement stressing the goals of peace, brotherhood and artistic expression.

As he explained to Englishman and anti-bullfight campaigner, Alfred Weirs, after the latter had paid the fine to release him, 'Fighting bulls are not allowed to mate. How doubly cruel it is that they should be killed never knowing what it is to make love'.

LEAST MAGICAL CASTLES

Dutch castles do not have the fairytale magic of many French chateaux or even English stately homes. 'In fact, they're kind of disappointing', confesses Paul Van Reyen, whose hobby and passion has been the study of medieval Dutch castles ever since objecting to the treatment of the subject in a Scandinavian text book.

Van Reyen dedicates his time off from work as a translator for a New Jersey stamp dealer to visiting, writing on and pestering the Dutch authorities about the misunderstood mansions.

Built mostly by minor – often extremely minor – nobility Holland's 300 surviving castles are what Van Reyen describes as 'very small'. People who have seen other country's castles, he says, are not impressed by them.

MOST SOLITARY SPORTSMAN

Lewis Sutter spent the swinging 'sixties playing solitaire. By 1971, he had played over 150,000 games in ten years, logging the results of his forty games a day in six giant ledgers.

Confessed Sutter, seventy-one, 'Solitaire doesn't interest me that much. But I can't think of anything else to do'.

MOST UNDERWHELMING WIMBLEDON CELEBRATION

Charlotte Cooper won her first Wimbledon singles final in 1892. After the match she cycled back to Surbiton where she was lodging with her brother.

She found him in the garden pruning his roses. Noticing that his sister looked fatigued, Dr Cooper asked, 'What have you been doing Chattie?'

'I've just won the championship', she told him.

Whereupon Dr Cooper made no reply but continued his pruning.

LEAST ACTION-PACKED CRICKET MATCH

Journalist Godfrey Smith tells the story of Groucho Marx being taken to his first cricket match. For the first half hour of play Marx sat transfixed. Finally, his companion turned to ask how he was enjoying the game. 'Fine', replied Groucho, 'when does it start?'

LEAST GLITTERING PRIZE

The thousand address stickers received by Northants woman, Sheila Guilford as winner of a recent know-your-postcode competition may sound nothing to go shouting from the rooftops about. But hers was a glittering prize indeed compared to the trophy dangled before entrants of a 1974 Grangemouth local authority competition to find the best filled form in the local census.

'The neatest household', explained an official, 'will win a free pencil. We feel this will be an attractive prize as many houses these days do not have one.'

MOST VICTIMIZED FOOTBALL FAN

Yet another example of the persecution of the dull came during the 1978 World Cup. It was the second week of the tournament and French fan and dull martyr, M. Trichard was well into his stride and on course for a 100 per cent viewing record, having seen every game screened so far.

When his wife therefore had the insensitivity to ask him in the middle of a match to help her prepare some peas for dinner, he explained that he was watching the World Cup and did not want to be disturbed. So she took down the family gun and shot him.

DULLEST HOBBY INVOLVING SHEEP

Listening to sheep graze may not sound as glamorous a hobby as say, hunting shark or shooting rhino.

But, says writer and sheep-listener Jackie Gillot, it is not a pastime without its own challenges. As she explained to readers of *The Listener* magazine in 1980:

> I lay down in a wet field last week to listen to the sound of sheep grazing. It is not an easy matter. First, the silly creatures bound away. Next, they remain rooted at some distance, staring not grazing.
>
> But after an hour their curiosity equalling mine, I was counterpointed by a quiet grazing.

DULL COLLECTING

Dull folks are great collectors.

But, on the principle that there is only so much modern art to go round, they collect stamps and coins but not Hockneys or Warhols.

They collect beer mats, Esso station special offer crystal, jumble sale rummage and, often, bits of string too short to be of any other use – but not ivory backgammon sets, sterling cocaine spoons or vintage Ferraris.

Some of the great dull collections of recent years include:

Earthiest collection

Victor Dormer, a carpenter from Croydon, collects mud. His specialty is Thames mud. 'There is a thousand years of history in Thames silt', he told reporters in 1981.

For this reason, however, Thames mud is also sought after by fellow collectors. At the time, Mr Dormer had barely 100 bags of it left. 'I shall have to go to Norfolk for some more', he said.

Smelliest collection

Celestine Pagliano of Savona, Italy collected dustbins. By 1964 when police answered complaints from neighbours about the smell coming from his house he had collected over 200, all full of rubbish.

'The collection was my pride', said Pagliano. 'I just wanted a hobby like everyone else'.

Canniest collection

Dorset man, Richard White collects taxes at work and beer cans at home. He has over 5,000 cans in his loft alone. If he brings home any more his wife has said they'll have to move.

'I have never liked beer', he says. He therefore bores a hole in the cans he buys and drains the contents.

He started collecting over ten years ago and set up the British Beer Can Society a little over five. Though his collection of British cans is unrivalled he is not interested in foreign cans, and trades any he gets.

One of the prides of his collection is a Temporary Tennents, made during the three-day week. It has written on it, 'This is a temporary can'. 'Not many of them were produced', he enthuses.

He does not worry about his collection being stolen. Who would want a pile of old beer cans?, he reasons.

Coldest collection

Canadian William Cheetey spent the 1960s collecting snow. By the end of what had, by all reports, been a good decade for snow, he had collected eight freezer-fulls, one for every winter from 1961.

The one drawback of the hobby, he said, was the cost of the electricity. 'But it's worth it for the pleasure it gives'.

Most topping collection

Arthur Jordan, a retired shipbuilder from Virginia, collects ring pull tops from drink cans. When counted in 1979 he had over 700,000 of them, enough to make a ring pull top necklace 11 miles long.

Holiest collection

Bobby Baxton of Atlanta, Georgia collects manhole covers. Or did, until 1956 when a court granted his wife Georgia a divorce after he started storing the smellier specimens from his 240-strong collection under her dressing table.

Most cut-and-tied collection

Minnesota man Francis Johnson collects string. After more than 30 years of the hobby, he has amassed a ball weighing five tons.

Baggiest collection

Englishwoman Bali Senn spent her childhood collecting brown paper bags, which she enjoyed spending long hours ironing. She had hoarded an impressive collection by the time her parents used them to move house and then, in her absence, threw them out.

Dullest last words

'I am about to – or, I am going to – die; either expression is used.'
Grammarian, Dominique Bonhours